Théodule A. Ribot

The Psychology of Attention

authorised translation

Théodule A. Ribot

The Psychology of Attention
authorised translation

ISBN/EAN: 9783337186982

Printed in Europe, USA, Canada, Australia, Japan

Cover: Foto ©Thomas Meinert / pixelio.de

More available books at **www.hansebooks.com**

THE

PSYCHOLOGY OF ATTENTION.

BY

TH. RIBOT,

PROFESSOR OF COMPARATIVE AND EXPERIMENTAL PSYCHOLOGY AT THE COLLEGE
DE FRANCE, EDITOR OF THE "REVUE PHILOSOPHIQUE."

AUTHORISED TRANSLATION.

CHICAGO:

THE OPEN COURT PUBLISHING COMPANY
169 La Salle Street
1890.

Je vous autorise
entièrement à publier cette traduction
et l'éditeur (M. Alcan) y consent
également

Th. Ribot

TABLE OF CONTENTS.

THE PSYCHOLOGY OF ATTENTION.

INTRODUCTORY.

PSYCHOLOGISTS have given much study to the effects of attention, but very little to its mechanism. The latter point is the only one that I propose to investigate in the following work. Yet even within these limits the question is important, for it is, as we shall later see, the counterpart, the necessary complement of the theory of association. If the present treatise contributes, however so little, to point out clearly this want of contemporaneous psychology, and to induce others to supply it, it will have accomplished its purpose.

Without attempting at present to define or to characterize attention, I shall take for granted that every one sufficiently understands what the term means. It is a matter of much greater difficulty to know at what point attention begins, and where it ends ; for it embraces all degrees from the transient instant accorded to the buzzing of a fly, to the state of complete absorption. It will be conformable to the rule of a sound method only to study cases that are marked and typical ; that is to say, those which present at least one of the following two characteristics : intensity and duration. When both these coincide, attention is at its maximum. Duration alone reaches the same result through accumulation : as, for instance, when one de-

ciphers a word or a figure by the light of several elec-
trical sparks.   Intensity alone is equally efficacious :
thus a woman will take in, in the twinkling of an eye,
the complete toilet of a rival.   The feeble forms of
attention can teach us nothing : at all events, it is not
from these that we must begin our study.   Before we
have yet traced the broad outlines of our work, it
would be idle to note the more delicate aspects, and
to waste time with subtile differences.   The purpose
of this series of essays is to establish and prove the
following propositions :

There are two well-defined forms of attention : the
one spontaneous, natural ; the other voluntary, artificial. The former—neglected by most psychologists—
is the true, primitive, and fundamental form of attention. The second—the only investigated by most psychologists—is but an imitation, a result of education,
of training, and of impulsion. Precarious and vacillating
in nature, it derives its whole being from spontaneous
attention, and finds only in the latter a point of support.   It is merely an apparatus formed by cultivation,
and a product of civilization.

Attention, in these two forms, is not an indetermi-
nate activity, a kind of "pure act" of spirit, acting by
mysterious and undiscoverable means.   Its mechanism is essentially *motory*, that is, it always acts upon
the muscles, and through the muscles, mainly under
the form of inhibition ; and as epigraph of this study
we might choose the words of Maudsley, that "the
person who is unable to control his own muscles, is incapable of attention." Attention, under these two forms,
is an exceptional, abnormal state, which cannot last a
long time, for the reason that it is in contradiction
to the basic condition of psychic life ; namely, change.

Attention is a state that is fixed. If it is prolonged beyond a reasonable time, particularly under unfavorable conditions, everybody knows from individual experience, that there results a constantly increasing cloudiness of the mind, finally a kind of intellectual vacuity, frequently accompanied by vertigo. These light, transient perturbations denote the radical antagonism of attention and the normal psychical life. The progress toward unity of consciousness, which is the very basis of attention, manifests itself still better in clearly morbid cases, which we shall study later under their chronic form, namely, the 'fixed idea,' and in their acute form, which is ecstacy.

Already from this point, without passing beyond generalities, we are able by the aid of this clearly marked characteristic—the tendency toward unity of consciousness—to reach a definition of attention. If we take any adult person, in good health, and of average intelligence, the ordinary mechanism of his mental life will consist in a perpetual coming and going of inward events, in a marching by of sensations, feelings, ideas, and images, which associate with, or repel, each other according to certain laws. Properly speaking, it is not, as frequently has been said, a chain, a series, but it is rather an irradiation in various directions, and through various strata ; a mobile aggregate which is being incessantly formed, unformed, and re-formed. Every one knows that this mechanism has been carefully studied in our day, and that the theory of association forms one of the solidest acquisitions of modern psychology. Not, indeed, that everything has been done ; for, in our opinion, the part sustained by the emotional states has not been sufficiently taken into account as the latent cause of a great number of associa-

tions.   More than once it happens that an idea evokes
another, not by virtue of a resemblance which would
be common to them in their character as ideas, but
because there is a common emotional fact which envel-
ops* and unites them.   There would thus remain the
task of reducing the laws of association to physiological laws, and the psychological mechanism to the cerebral mechanism that supports it; but we are still
very far from this ideal point.

The normal condition is plurality of states of consciousness, or—according to the expression employed
by ceitain authors — polyideism.   Attention is the
momentary inhibition, to the exclusive benefit of a
single state, of this perpetual progression : it is a
monoideism.   But it is necessary clearly to determine,
in what sense we use this term.   Is attention a reduction to a sole and single state of consciousness?   No ;
for inward observation teaches us, that it is only a
relative monoideism; that is, it supposes the existence
of a master-idea, drawing to itself all that relates to
it, and nothing else, allowing associations to produce
themselves only within very narrow limits, and on
condition that they converge toward a common point.
It drains for its own use—at least in the proportion
possible—the entire cerebral activity.

Do there really exist cases of *absolute* monoideism,
in which consciousness is reduced to a sole and single
state entirely occupying it, and in which the mechanism
of association is totally arrested ?   In our opinion, this
we meet in only a few, very rare cases of ecstacy,
which we shall analyze later on ; still it is for a fleeting
instant only, because consciousness disappears when

* See good instances in J. Sully: " Illusions," Chap. VII

placed beyond the conditions that are rigorously necessary to its existence.

Attention (we here once more and for the last time recall the fact, that we shall only study the clearest cases) consists accordingly in the substitution of a relative unity of consciousness for the plurality of states, for the change which constitutes the rule. Yet this does not suffice to define attention. A very bad toothache, a nephritic colic, or intense enjoyment produce a momentary unity of consciousness, which we do not confuse with attention proper. Attention has an object ; it is not a purely subjective modification : it is a cognition, an intellectual state. This is an additional characteristic to be noted.

This is not all. To distinguish it from certain states which approach it, and which will be studied in the course of our work (for example, fixed ideas), we must take account of the adaptation that always accompanies it, and which, as we shall attempt to establish, in a great measure constitutes its character. In what does this adaptation consist ? For the present, let us limit ourselves to an entirely superficial view.

In cases of spontaneous attention, the whole body converges toward its object, the eyes, ears, and sometimes the arms ; all motions are arrested. Our personality is captured, that is, all the tendencies of the individual, all his available energy aim at the same point. The physical and external adaptation is a sign of psychic and inward adaptation. Convergence is a reduction to unity substituting itself for that diffusion of movements and attitudes which characterizes the normal state.

In cases of voluntary attention adaptation is most

frequently incomplete, intermittent, without solidity.
The movements are inhibited, yet to reappear from
time to time. The organism converges, but in a
languid, reluctant sort of way. Intermissions of physical adaptation are a sign of intermissions of mental
adaptation. The personality has been only partly
won, and at intermittent moments.

I must ask the reader to pardon the circumstance
that these brief remarks are somewhat obscure and
insufficient. Details and proofs will come later. It
was merely a question of paving the way for a definition of attention which, I believe, I can present in
the following form : " It is an intellectual monoideism,
accompanied by spontaneous or artificial adaptation of
the individual." Or, if we prefer another formula :
"Attention consists in an intellectual state, exclusive
or predominant, with spontaneous or artificial adaptation of the individual."

But let us now leave the foregoing generalities, in
order to study, in their mechanism, the several forms
of attention.

CHAPTER I.

SPONTANEOUS ATTENTION.

I.

SPONTANEOUS attention is the only existing form of
attention until education and artificial means have
been employed. There exists no other kind in most
animals and in young children. It is a gift of nature,
but very unequally distributed among individuals.
Still, whether strong or weak, everywhere and always
it is caused by emotional states. This rule is absolute,
without exception. Man, like animals, lends his at-

tention spontaneously only to what concerns and in-
terests him; to what produces in him an agreeable, disagreeable, or mixed state.   As pleasure and pain are
only signs that certain of our tendencies are being satisfied or crossed; and as our tendencies are what is
deepest in us; as they express the very depths of our
personality, of our character; it follows that spontaneous attention has its roots in the very basis of our being.
The nature of spontaneous attention in any person re-
veals his character, or, at least, his fundamental tendencies.   It tells us, whether a person is frivolous,
vulgar, narrow, open, or deep.   The janitor's wife will
spontaneously lend her whole attention to the gossip
of her neighbors; the painter to a beautiful sunset, in
which the peasant only sees the approach of night;
the geologist to the stones he chances to find, in which
the uninitiated only see worthless pebbles.   Let the
reader look into himself and around him; the examples are so easily found, that it is useless to dwell
longer upon them here.

It might be a subject of wonder that so evident and
striking a truth (for spontaneous attention without an
anterior emotional state would be an effect without a
cause) should not long ago have been recognized as a
common acquisition of psychology, if indeed the majority of psychologists had not obstinately persevered
in the exclusive study of the higher forms of attention,
that is to say, in beginning at the end.*   It is highly
necessary, on the contrary, to dwell upon its primitive

---

* The psychologists who have clearly seen the importance of the emo-
tional states in attention, are so few, that I am only able to quote Maudsley,
"Physiology of Mind," Chap. V; Lewes, "Problems of Life and Mind,"
Vol. III, p. 184; Carpenter, "Mental Physiology," Chap. III; Horwiez, "*Psy-
chologische Analysen*," Chap. I, and a few of Herbart's disciples, particularly
Volkmar, "*Lehrbuch der Psychologie*," Vol. II, Sec. 114.

form : without the latter nothing is intelligible, nothing
explainable, everything is vague, and we should remain without the guiding thread of our study.   Accordingly, we shall not hesitate to multiply the number
of our proofs.

Any man or animal, hypothetically incapable of
experiencing either pleasure or pain, would be incapable of attention.   There could only exist for him
certain states more intense than certain other ones,
which is an entirely different matter.   It is accordingly
impossible to maintain, in the same sense as Condillac,
that if amid a multitude of sensations, there is one
that predominates by its intensity, it is therewith
"transformed into attention."   It is not intensity alone
that acts, but, above all, our adaptation, that is to say,
our tendencies, as they happen to be crossed or satisfied.   Intensity is but an element, and oftentimes
the least important.   Thus we may observe how spontaneous attention is natural and devoid of effort.   The
idler, who loafs around in the street, will stare with
gaping mouth at a procession or passing masquerade,
and preserve perfect imperturbability so long as the
procession lasts.   If at any time effort appears, it is a
sign that attention changes in character, that it becomes voluntary, artificial.

In the biographies of great men, traits abound,
which prove, that spontaneous attention entirely depends upon emotional states.   These traits are the
best, because they show us the phenomenon in all its
force.   Instances of great attention are always caused
and sustained by great passions.   Fourier, says Arago,
remained turbulent and incapable of application until
his thirteenth year : he was then initiated into the
elements of mathematics, and forthwith became a dif-

ferent man. Malebranche, by chance, reluctantly takes up Descartes's treatise "*de l'Homme*"; the perusal of it "caused such a violent beating of the heart that from hour to hour he was compelled to lay the book aside, and break off its perusal, in order to breathe freely"; and he becomes a Cartesian. It is useless to speak of Newton, and many others. Some perhaps will say : Such traits are the marks of a dawning voca- tion. But what indeed is a vocation but attention, discovering its way, its true bearings for the rest of life? No finer instances of spontaneous attention could be given, for this form does not last for only a few minutes or an hour, but forever.

Let us examine a different aspect of the question. Is the state of attention continuous? Yes, apparently so ; but in reality, it is intermittent. "What is called giving attention to one thing, is, strictly speaking, the following a *series* of impressions or connected ideas, with an ever renewed and deepening interest. For ex- ample, when we witness a dramatic representation.... And even a prolonged attention to a small material ob- ject, as a coin, or a flower, involves a continual tran- sition of mind from one aspect to another, one set of suggestions to another. Hence it would be more cor- rectly described as making the object the *centre* of at- tention, the point from which it sets out and to which it continually reverts." *

Researches in psycho-physics, of which we shall speak later (Chap. II, Sec. 4), show that attention is subject to the law of rhythm. Stanley Hall, while study- ing with great care the gradual changes of pressure pro- duced upon the tips of the fingers, has established the fact, that the perception of continuity seems impos-

* J. Sully, Outlines of Psychology. Chap. IV.

sible, and that the subject cannot have the feeling of continuous augmentation or decrease.

Attention chooses between different degrees of pressure, in order to compare them. Certain errors in the notation of astronomical phenomena are also due to these oscillations of attention. *

Maudsley and Lewes have compared attention to a reflex motion; it would be more proper to say, a series of reflexes. Any physical excitation produces a movement. Similarly a stimulation coming from the object produces an incessantly repeated adaptation. Deep and tenacious cases of spontaneous attention have all the characteristics of unassuaged passion, which unceasingly re-commences in the effort to satisfy itself. The dipsomaniac, before a filled glass, will swallow its contents; and if some malignant fairy, as soon as it was emptied, refilled it, he would never stop. Erotic passion acts in like manner. Vicq d'Azyr maintained that monkeys could not be trained, because they cannot be made attentive (which in the first place, is not true). To this Gall retorted: Show a monkey its female, and you will find out whether it is capable of attention. When confronting any scientific problem, the Newtonian mind acts in the same manner; it falls a prey to a perpetual irritation, which holds it in its power without cessation or rest. No fact is clearer, more incontestable, more easily verified than this, namely, that spontaneous attention depends upon emotional states, such as desires, satisfaction, discontent, jealousy, etc.; its intensity and its duration depend upon their intensity and their duration.

Let us here note a fact of considerable importance

---

* "American Journal of Psychology," 1887, No. 1. "Philosophische Studien," 1888, Vol. V, p. 56, and following.

in the mechanism of attention. This real intermission
in an apparent continuity alone renders possible any
long attention. If we keep one of our eyes fixed upon
any single point, after a while our vision becomes
confused ; a cloud is formed between the object and
ourselves, and finally we see nothing at all. If we lay
our hand flat upon a table, motionless, and without
pressure (for pressure itself is a movement), by slow
degrees the sensation wears off, and finally disappears.
The reason is, that there is no perception without
movement, be it ever so weak. Every sensorial organ
is at the same time both sensitive and motory. As
soon as absolute immobility eliminates one of the two
elements (motility), the function of the other after a
while is rendered null. In a word, movement is the
condition of the change, which is one of the conditions
of consciousness. These well-known facts, of common
experience, make us understand the necessity of these
intermissions in attention, often imperceptible to consciousness, because they are very brief, and of a very
delicate order.

II.

THE physical manifestations of attention are numerous and of very great importance. We shall minutely pass them in review, while forewarning the
reader, that we consider them less as effects of this
state of mind, than as its necessary conditions—frequently even as its constitutive elements. This study,
accordingly, far from being subordinate to our purpose, is really an investigation of capital importance.
To obtain an approximately clear idea of the mechanism of attention, we shall not have to look anywhere
else. It is, in fact, only an attitude of the mind, a

purely formal state ; if we divest it of all the physical concomitants that determine and give it substance, we remain in the presence of a pure abstraction, a phantom.   And so the psychologists that have only spoken of attention from inward observation, have remained silent concerning its mechanism, and have limited themselves to extolling its power.

It is always necessary to bear in mind the following fundamental principle : Every intellectual state is accompanied by definite physical manifestations. Thought is not,—as many from tradition still admit,—an event taking place in a purely super-sensual, ethereal, inaccessible world.   We shall repeat with Setchenoff, ''No thought without expression '' ; that is, thought is a word or an act in a nascent state, that is to say, a commencement of muscular activity.   The sensorial forms of attention so clearly testify to this principle that it cannot be questioned.   The same applies to that internal, hidden process, called reflection, of which we shall speak later.

The physical concomitants of attention can be referred to three groups : vaso-motor phenomena, respiratory phenomena, and motory phenomena, or phenomena of expression.   They all denote a state of convergence of the organism and of concentration of labor.

I. Let us suppose that twenty persons fix their attention for five or ten minutes upon their little finger. In such case something like the following will happen. Some will be unconscious of any sensation whatever ; others will experience certain distinct sensations, as suffering, pain, arterial pulsations ; the majority will feel a faint impression of heaviness and a crawling sensation.   This simple experiment raises the following questions : Do there not always exist in the several

parts of the body sensations, due to incessant modifications of the tissues—modifications which pass by unperceived unless attention is fixed upon the same?
Can the act of attention increase the vascular activity
of the sensorial ganglia, and there produce subjective sensations? Finally, can the sympathetic centres
be aroused, can the vaso-motory nerves be so influenced
as to produce certain transitory vascular modifications in the finger with which the sensation is connected?

The first supposition seems probable only to a very
slight degree. Indeed, it is always possible to experience a sensation in the finger, if we set about attentively to seek for this sensation.

But, we think that the two other suppositions are
perfectly well grounded. The sensation experienced
is perhaps partially subjective ; but in our opinion, the
finger, upon which thought is concentrated for a sufficient space of time, is really the seat of a sensation.
The vascular modifications that take place, are felt in
the form of arterial pulsations, heaviness, etc.*

It is highly probable, and almost universally admitted, that attention, even when not directed toward
any region of our body, is accompanied by local hyper-
hæmia of certain parts of the brain. The vascu-
larization of the parts concerned, increases in consequence of greater functional activity. This local hy-
perhæmia is caused by a dilatation of the arteries,
which itself is caused by the action of the vaso-motor
nerves upon the muscular integuments of the arteries.
The vaso-motor nerves depend on the great sympathetic nerve, which is independent of the action of the
will, but which is subjected to all the influences of the

* Hack Tuke, " Mind and Body," p. 2.

emotional states. The experiments of Mosso, among others, show that the slightest and most transient emotion causes an afflux of blood to the brain. "There is," says Maudsley, "a more active circulation of blood through the brain during function than when it is in repose. We may fairly conclude, then, that the effect of attention to a current of thought is to quicken the circulation in the nervous substrata which minister to it; not otherwise than as when some earnest thought has taken hold of the mind, it keeps up an active circulation in the brain, and will not let us go to sleep."* After a spell of protracted attention we may also notice the redness (sometimes the pallor) of the face.

II. The respiratory modifications which accompany attention resemble the motor phenomena proper, and enter partly into the feeling of effort. The rhythm of respiration changes, slackens, and sometimes undergoes a temporary stoppage. "To acquire the power of attention," says Lewes, "is to learn to make our mental adjustments alternate with the rhythmic movements of respiration. It is a felicitous expression, that in the French language, which designates a clever but superficial thinker, as one incapable of any work *de longue haleine*—of long breath."† The yawning which follows a protracted effort of attention is probably the effect of the slackening of respiration. Often, in like instances, we produce a prolonged inhalation, in order to renew abundantly the air within our lungs. The sigh—another respiratory symptom—as several authors have pointed out, is common to attention, to

---

* Maudsley: "Physiology of Mind." Gley: *Sur l'etat du pouls carotidien pendant le travail intellectuel.*

† Consult Lewes, loc. cit., p. 188.

physical, and moral pain : its object is to oxygenize the blood that has been narcotized by the voluntary or involuntary stoppage of respiration.

All these facts are so many proofs in support of what has been said before, that attention is an exceptional, abnormal fact, which cannot last a long time.

III. The movements of the body, which are said to express attention, are also of paramount importance. In this chapter we can only enter into a partial study of the same ; the remainder will be more properly studied under the title of voluntary attention :* but here, for the first time, we shall proceed to investigate the motory mechanism of attention.

In the first place let us examine the facts. They have not been seriously studied before our own time. Formerly only artists and a few physiognomists—both at all times too partial to their own fancies—had concerned themselves about them.

Duchenne, of Boulogne,—a pioneer in this as in various other fields,—conceived the idea of substituting the experimental method for the pure observation practiced by his predecessors, Ch. Bell, Gratiolet, etc.   By the aid of electricity he provoked the isolated contraction of a facial muscle of a man affected with anæsthesia, and by means of photography he obtained the results of the experiment.   According to the theory which he had set forth in his *Mécanisme de la physionomie humaine* (1862), a slight contraction of a single muscle is often sufficient to express an emotion ; every emotional state produces a single local modification. Thus, according to him, the occipito-frontalis is the muscle of attention ; the orbicularis superior of the eye-lids, the muscle of reflection ; the pyramidal, the muscle of

* See Chap. II. *infra.*

menace; the zygomaticus major, the muscle of laughter ;
the eye-brow-muscle, the muscle of grief ; the triangular
of the lips, the muscle of contempt ; and so on.   Still,
Duchenne limited himself to stating merely the facts ; in
this following the example of J. Müller, who declared
that the expression of the emotions is a completely in-
explicable fact.   Darwin went still further.   Making
use of the comparative method, and relying upon
laborious researches, he investigated the origin of the
different mechanisms of expression ; he tried hard to
establish why the contraction of a certain given muscle
of the face, is necessarily associated with a certain
given state of mind.

In the absence of these minute investigations all
attempts to explain the mechanism of attention would
have been premature.   How, indeed, is it possible to
explain a mechanism, the wheel-work of which is unknown to us?   Let us see, in a summary way, what
we know concerning attention in its two forms ; as
applied to external objects (attention proper), or to
internal events (reflection).

Attention (in order to mark it more precisely, we
shall call it sensorial) contracts the occipitio-frontalis.
This muscle, which occupies the whole region of the
forehead, has its mobile point of insertion in the under
surface of the skin of the eye-brow and its fixed point
of insertion at the back part of the skull.   In contracting, it draws to itself the eyebrow, lifts it, and
produces a few transversal wrinkles on the forehead ;
consequently the eye is wide open and well illuminated.
In extreme cases the mouth opens wide.   In children
and in many adults close attention produces a protru-
sion of the lips, a kind of pouting.   Preyer has attempted to explain this facial play by hereditary in-

fluence. "All animals," he says, "first direct their attention to the search for food. The objects that their lips, their feelers, their proboscis, and their tongue can reach, are those with reference to which their first investigations are made. All examination of, and all search for, food, consequently, is accompanied by a preponderative activity of the mouth and of its appendants. In suckling, the mouth of the infant protrudes forward." In this manner an association would be formed between the first movements of the mouth and the activity of attention.

The act of reflection is expressed in another, and almost contrary manner. It acts on the superior orbicular muscle of the eye-lids and lowers the eye-brow. As a consequence, small vertical folds are formed in the space between the eye-brows : the eye is veiled or completely closed, or it looks within. This wrinkling of the eye-brows imparts to the face an expression of intellectual energy. The mouth is closed, as if to sustain an effort.

Attention adapts itself to what is without, reflection to what is within. Darwin explains by an analogy the mode in which reflection expresses itself. It is the attitude of difficult vision, transferred from external objects to internal events that are difficult to grasp.* Hitherto we have only spoken of the movements of the face ; but there are, besides these, those of the entire body—of the head, trunk, and limbs. It is impossible to describe them in detail, because they vary with each animal species.† In general a state of

---

* For details see: Darwin, "Expression of the Emotions," Chap. X ; Preyer, "The Mind of the Child," p. 250, et seqq. ; Montegazza, " La physio-nomie," Chap. XVI.

† An excellent study of the expression of attention in animals will be found in Ricardi, "Saggio di studi e di osservazioni interno all' attenzione nell' nomo e negli animali." Modena, 1877, (second part, p. 1-17).

immobility sets in, adaptation of eyes, ears, and of touch, as the case may happen : in a word, there is a tendency toward unity of action—convergence. Concentration of consciousness, and concentration of movements, diffusion of ideas and diffusion of movements go together. Let us recall the observations and calculations of Galton upon this subject. He observed an audience of fifty persons, listening to a long and tiresome lecture. The number of movements clearly discernible in the audience was very uniform : forty-five a minute, or, say an average of one movement for each person. Several times, the attention of the audience having been aroused, the number of movements decreased by one half; besides they were less extended, less prolonged, shorter and more rapid. I may incidentally anticipate an objection. Everybody knows that attention, at least, in its reflected form, is at times accompanied by movements. Many people seem to find that walking to and fro helps them out of perplexity; others strike their forehead, scratch their head, rub their eyes, move their arms and legs about in an incessant, rhythmical fashion. This, indeed, is an expenditure, not an economy of motion. But it is a profitable expenditure. The movements thus produced are not simple mechanical phenomena, acting upon our external surroundings; they act also through the muscular sense upon the brain, which receives them as it receives all other sensorial impressions, to the increase of the brain's activity. A rapid walk, a race, will also quicken the flow of ideas and words ; they produce, as Bain says, a sort of mechanical intoxication. The experimental researches of M. Féré, which we cannot quote here,* furnish nu-

* See his book, " Sensation and Movement."

merous instances of the dynamogenetic action of movements. We stretch out our arms and legs to begin work ; that is, we arouse the motor centres. Passive movements impressed upon paralyzed members, have in certain cases, been able, by reviving motory images, to restore lost activity. And it is to be observed, that the result of these movements is to increase mental activity, and not to concentrate the attention ; they simply provide it with subject-matter. It is a preliminary operation only.

We must now determine the real part sustained by the movements in attention. Up to this point we have limited ourselves to describing them—at least the principal ones ; we are now prepared to put the question in its clearest and simplest terms :

Are the movements of the face, the body, and the limbs, and the respiratory modifications that accompany attention, simply effects, outward marks, as is usually supposed ? Or, are they, on the contrary, *the necessary conditions, the constituent elements, the indispensable factors of attention ?* Without hesitation we accept the second thesis. Totally suppress movements, and you totally suppress attention.

Although for the time being we are in a position only partially to establish the point maintained (the study of voluntary attention, reserved for an other chapter, will show it to us in a new aspect), still since we are now touching upon the essential feature of the mechanism of attention, it seems proper to dwell awhile upon the subject.

The fundamental rôle of the movements in attention is, to *maintain* the appropriate state of consciousness and to *reinforce* it. But as this is a question of mechanism, it will be preferable to approach the

problem from its physiological side, by an inquiry into
what takes place in the brain, in its double capacity of
an intellectual and a motory organ.

1. As an intellectual organ the brain serves as sub-
stratum to perceptions (in sensorial attention), images,
and ideas (in reflection).   By hypothesis, the nervous
elements that act will furnish, on an average, a
superior work.

Attention certainly causes an intense innervation,
as proved by the numerous experiments of psychom-
etry, in which it plays a part.   "An active idea," says
Maudsley, "is accompanied by a molecular change in
the nervous elements, which is propagated either along
the sensory nerve to its periphery, or, if not so far, at
any rate to the sensory ganglion, the sensibility of
which is thereby increased.   The result of this propagation of molecular action to the ganglion is that the
different muscles in connection with the affected sense
are put into a certain tension by reflex action, and
thereby increase the feeling of attention, in accordance
with the law that associated feelings strengthen one
another."* Attention, according to Hartmann, " consists in material vibrations of the nerves," in a nerve-
current, which, traversing the sensible nerves, proceeds from centre to periphery.†   But there is another
element of equal importance.

2. As a motor organ the brain plays a complex
rôle.   In the first place, it inaugurates the movements
that accompany perceptions, images, or ideas ; afterwards, these movements, which frequently are intense,
return to the brain by way of the muscular sense as
sensations of movements ;   the latter increase the

* Loc. cit., p. 313.
†*Philosophie de l'inconscient, trad. Nolen*, Vol. I, p. 145; Vol. II, p. 65

quantity of available energy, which on the one hand serves to maintain or to reinforce consciousness, and, on the other, returns to its original starting-point in the form of a fresh movement.

In this manner there is a constant going and coming from centre to periphery, from periphery to centre, and from the strengthened centre again to periphery, etc.   The intensity of consciousness is but the subjective expression of this complicated work.   But to suppose that this state could last without these organic conditions, is an untenable hypothesis, completely in disaccord with all that experience teaches us.   The naïve spectator at the Opera, who is bored at the unintelligibility of the music, is all attention when a sudden change of scenery occurs; that is, when the visual impression has produced an instantaneous adaptation of the eyes and the whole body. Without this organic convergence the impression would rapidly vanish.   " The difference between attention and voluntary movement," says Wundt, "consists essentially in the preponderant reaction upon the sensitive parts (the original source of the performance). In voluntary movement, the main direction of the central excitation is toward the muscles; in attention, the muscles only act in conjunction with subordinate, sympathetic movements" ; * or, in other terms, a reflection of movements is produced.   Finally, in the words of Maudsley, we may declare the mechanism of attention to be : "first, the excitation of the proper ideational track either by external presentation or internal representation ; secondly, the intensification of its energy by the increment of stimulus resulting from the

* *Physiologische Psychologie*, pp. 723-724 of the first edition. This passage is not found in the following editions.

proper motor innervation ; thirdly, a further intensification of energy by the subsequent reaction of the
more active perceptive centre upon the motor factor—
the interplay of sensory and motor factors augment-
ing the activity up to a certain limit."*

If, accordingly, we compare the ordinary state with
the state of attention, we find in the former weak rep-
resentations, and but few movements; but in the
latter, a vivid representation, energetic, and conver-
gent movements, and moreover repercussion of the
movements produced.   It matters little, whether this
last addition be conscious or not : consciousness does
not perform the operation ; it simply profits by it.

It may perhaps be interposed that, admitting this
reaction of the movements upon the brain, still there
is nothing to prove that the movements are originally
the simple effect of attention.   There are three hypotheses possible, namely: either, attention (the state of
consciousness) is the cause of the movements, or it is
the effect of the same, or it is first the cause and afterwards the effect of the movements.

Still, I do not wish to choose between these three
hypotheses which have a purely logical and dialectic
import, but rather to put the question otherwise.   In
the above-stated form the problem is thoroughly im-
pregnated—without appearing to be so—with that
traditional dualism, of which psychology finds it so
difficult to rid itself ; and the problem is reduced, in
effect, to the question, whether in attention the soul first
acts upon the body or the body upon the soul.   This
enigma is not for me to solve.   To the eye of physiological psychology there exist only internal states, differing among each other as well by their peculiar qualities

* Loc. cit., p. 316.

as by their physical concomitants. If the intellectual state produced is weak, brief, without perceptible expression, then it is not attention. If it is strong, stable, well-defined, and marked by the before-mentioned physical modifications, then it is attention. The point here maintained is, that attention does not exist *in abstracto*, as a purely inward event: it is a concrete state, a psycho-physiological complex. Take our spectator at the opera. Abstract from him the adaptation of eyes, head, body, limbs, changes of respiration and cerebral circulation, etc., and the conscious or unconscious reaction of all these phenomena upon the brain; and that which is left of the original whole, thus despoiled and emptied, is no longer attention. If anything remain, it is an ephemeral state of consciousness, the shadow of that which has been. We hope that this example, however far-fetched it may seem, will better contribute to an understanding of this point than long disquisitions. The motory manifestations are neither effects nor causes, but elements; together with the state of consciousness, which constitutes their subjective side, *they are* attention.

The reader, however, is not to regard this as anything more than a rough outline, or provisional view, that will be completed later on. Thus, we have not spoken of the feeling of effort, because it is very rare in spontaneous attention, if met with at all. But the part sustained by the movements is sufficiently important to justify repeated investigations of the subject.

III.

The state of surprise or astonishment is spontaneous attention augmented; a few words with reference to it are now in order. Although of frequent occurence in every-day life, it has been forgotten by psychology. I find, however, in the *Traité des passions* of Descartes (Part II, Art. 70) the following definition : "Admiration is a sudden surprise of the soul, which causes it to consider with attention those objects that to it appear unfrequent and extraordinary. Thus, in the first place, it is caused by the impression in our brain representing the object as rare, and consequently as worthy of exceptional consideration ; and in the second place by the movement of our thoughts, which by virtue of that impression are disposed to tend with great force toward the locality of the brain in which the impression rests, in order to strengthen and preserve it there ; as they are also disposed, through that impression, to pass from thence into the muscles that serve to maintain the sensory organs in the same position in which they are, in order that, if originally formed by the organs of sense, the impression may be further prolonged by their support." It will repay us, well to ponder this passage. If we carefully peruse it, we shall find that due allowance being made for slight differences of language, nearly all the elements which we have endeavored to point out in the mechanism of spontaneous attention, are therein clearly enumerated ; namely :—the augmentation of nervous influx in consequence of the impression ; its partial conduction toward the muscles ; the action of these muscles in order "to support" and "to strengthen." Incidentally we may remark, that Descartes's method of treatment is that of physiological psychology and not that of spiritualistic psychology, which quite improperly lays claim to him.

Surprise, and in a higher degree astonishment, is a shock produced by that which is new and unexpected ; as if, for example, a person who travels little and whom

I believe to be at home, some five or six hundred miles away, suddenly enters my room.

From the mental standpoint, there is little to be said of it. It belongs to the group of Emotions, and in its strong form, it is a commotion. Properly speaking, it is not so much a state, as an intermediate condition between two states, an abrupt rupture, a gap, an hiatus. At the moment of the shock the previous polyideism abruptly ends, because the new state rushes in, like a giant, into the struggle for life going on among the states of consciousness. By degrees the new state finds its place, is put into connection with others, and equilibrium tends to be re-established ; but surprise having passed away, the state that follows it is attention, that is, an adjusted monoideism— adaptation having had time to take place. The intellectual element regains the upper hand over the emotional element. It is highly probable, that in the state of surprise we have imperfect knowledge because we have too much sensation.

From the physical side the symptoms are an exaggeration of spontaneous attention. "Attention," as we have seen, "is shown by the eyebrows being slightly raised ; and as this state increases into surprise, they are raised to a much greater extent, with the eyes and mouth widely open. . . . . The degree to which the eyes and mouth are opened corresponds with the degree of surprise felt."* This raising of the eye-brows is an instinctive act ; because it is also met with in individuals born blind : it allows the eyes to be opened very rapidly. As to the opening of the

* Darwin 'The Expression of the Emotions' (Chap. XII). The probable origin of these diverse movements is discussed there.

mouth, it permits a vigorous and deep inspiration, which
we are always wont to make before any great effort.

We have said, that surprise is spontaneous attention augmented.   I believe that this assertion is perfectly allowable.   This state best exemplifies the emotional causes of spontaneous attention ; for, from the
latter there is an insensible gradation to surprise, to
astonishment, to stupefaction, and finally to fright and
to terror, which are emotional states of a very high
degree of intensity.

Brought back now to the point from which we
started, we are thus able to see, that the origin of
attention is very humble, and that its primitive forms
have actually been bound up with the most exacting
conditions of animal life.   Attention, from the first,
had but a biological value.   The habit of psychologists
to restrict themselves to voluntary attention and even
then to its higher manifestations, concealed its origin.

We may assert "a priori" that if attention is caused
by emotional states, which in their turn are caused by
tendencies, needs, and appetites, it is in its last analysis inseparably bound up with that which lies deepest in the individual—the instinct of self-preservation.

A rapid examination of the facts will enable us
better to see that the power of being attentive in the
struggle for life has been an advantage of the foremost
order ; but we must leave man and descend lower still—
indeed, very low—in the scale of animal life.   I leave
aside completely the rudimentary forms of psychic
life, which only too easily afford a pretext for con-
jectures and aberrations.   In order that attention can
be evoked, a few developed senses at least will be requisite, a few clear perceptions, and a competent motor
apparatus.   Riccardi, in his previously mentioned

work, finds the first clear expression of attention in *Arthropoda.*

Any animal so organized that the impressions of the external world were all of equal significance to it, in whose consciousness all impressions stood upon the same level, without any single one predominating or inducing an appropriate motory adaptation—were exceedingly ill-equipped for its own preservation. I shall overlook the extreme case, in which predominance and adaptation would favor detrimental impressions; for an animal thus constituted must perish, being an illogical organism—a kind of incorporate contradiction. The usual case remains, *viz.:* the predominance of useful sensations, that is, of those connected with nutrition, self-defence, and the propagation of the species. The impressions of prey to be caught, of an enemy to be avoided, and from time to time, of a female to be fecundated, become settled in the consciousness of the animal with their adapted movements. Attention, thus, is at the service of and dependent upon necessities; always connected with the sense most perfectly developed, the sense of touch, of sight, of hearing, of smelling, according to the species. Here attention is seen in all its simplicity, and here it affords the most instruction. It was necessary to descend to these rudimentary forms, in order to grasp the reason of its power:—attention is a condition of life; and it will preserve this identical character in its higher forms, where, ceasing to be a factor of adaptation in a purely physical environment it becomes, as we shall see, a factor of adaptation in the social environment. In all the forms of attention, from the lowest to the highest, there is *unity of composition.*

And besides, among the highest-class animals even,

attention loses its limited and material character. The great majority of animal species are enclosed within the narrow circle of feeding, propagating, sleeping ; in this their entire activity is expended. The most intelligent have a superfluous activity, which is expended in the form of play—a manifestation which is so important, that several authors have made play the original source of art. To this need of luxury there also corresponds an attention for luxury. Dogs, that their masters amuse in a certain manner, become attentive when they see the latter making preparations for the same game ; and a close observer of children, Sikorski, has shown that their activity and attention are mainly developed through play.*

* *Revue Philosophique*, April, 1885.

CHAPTER II.

VOLUNTARY ATTENTION.

Voluntary or artificial attention is a product of art, of education, of direction, and of training. It is grafted, as it were, upon spontaneous or natural attention, and finds in the latter its conditions of existence, as the graft does in the stock, into which it has been inserted. In spontaneous attention the object acts by its intrinsic power; in voluntary attention the subject acts through extrinsic, that is, through superadded powers. In voluntary attention the aim is no longer set by hazard or circumstances; it is willed, chosen, accepted or, at least, submitted to; it is mainly a question of adapting ourselves to it, and of finding the proper means for maintaining the state; and hence voluntary attention is always accompanied by a certain feeling of effort. The maximum of spontaneous attention and the maximum of voluntary attention are totally antithetic; the one running in the direction of the strongest attraction, the other in the direction of the greatest resistance. They constitute the two polar limits between which all possible degrees are found, with a definite point at which, in theory at least, the two forms meet.

Although voluntary attention is almost the only form that psychologists have studied, and though to the majority it constitutes all of attention, its mechanism, nevertheless, has not been any better understood. In attempting to arrive at some comprehension of it, we first propose to investigate how voluntary attention is formed, to inquire into its genesis; then we shall study the feeling of effort by which it is accompanied, and finally the phenomena of arrested motion or inhibition, which, in our opinion, play a principal part in the mechanism of attention.

I.

The process through which voluntary attention is formed, may be reduced to the following single formula: To render attractive, by artifice, what is not so by nature; to give an artificial interest to things that have not a natural interest.   I use the word "interest" in the ordinary sense, as equivalent to the periphrase : anything that keeps the mind on the alert.   But the mind is only kept alert by the agreeable, disagreeable, or mixed action of objects upon it, that is, by emotional states.   With this difference however, that here the feelings that sustain attention, are acquired, superadded, not spontaneous, as in its primitive manifestations. The whole question, accordingly, is reduced to the finding of effective motives; if the latter be wanting, voluntary attention does not appear.

Such is the process in general ; in practice, however, it becomes infinitely diversified.

In order properly to understand the genesis of voluntary attention, the best way will be to study children and the higher animals.   The simplest examples will prove the most instructive.

During the earliest period of its life the child is

only capable of spontaneous attention. It fixes its gaze only upon shining objects, and upon the faces of its mother or nurse. Toward the end of the third month it explores its field of vision, by degrees allowing its eyes to rest upon objects less and less interesting (Preyer). The same takes place in regard to the other senses ; there is a slow transition from that which is of greatest concern to that which is of least concern. The fixing of the gaze, which later becomes intense attention, is outwardly expressed by the more marked contraction of various muscles. Attention in the infant is accompanied by a certain emotional state, which Preyer calls 'the emotion of astonishment.' At its highest point, this state produces a temporary immobility of the muscles. According to Dr. Sikorski, "astonishment, or rather the emotion that accompanies the psychic process of attention, is chiefly characterized by the momentary suspension of respiration—a striking phenomenon indeed, after being accustomed to the rapid respiration of children."* It is almost impossible to tell, at what period the first appearance of will takes place. Preyer claims to have noticed indications of will toward the fifth month, but in its impulsive form ; as a power of inhibition it appears much later.

So long as the psychic life thus remains in the tentative epoch, attention, that is, the transfer of the mind from one object to another, is determined only by the objects' power of attraction. The birth of voluntary attention, the power of fastening the mind upon non-attractive objects, can only be accomplished by force, under the influence of education, whether de-

* Sikorski : " Le Développement psychique de l'Enfant. (Revue l'Philoso-phique, April, 1885.)

rived from men or things external. Education, derived from men, is, of course, the most easily demon-
strable, but it is not the only kind.

A child refuses to learn how to read ; it is incapable
of keeping its mind fixed upon letters that have no attraction for it; but it will gaze with eagerness upon
pictures in a book. "What do those pictures mean?"
Its father answers : "When you know how to read, the
book will tell you." After a few talks of this kind
the child finally gives up ; at first it sets about the
task lazily, but afterwards it becomes accustomed to its
work, and finally evinces an eagerness that needs to
be checked. In this we have an instance of the genesis of voluntary attention. It was necessary to graft
upon a desire natural and direct, a desire artificial
and indirect. Reading is an operation that does not
possess an immediate attraction, but as a means to an
end it has an attraction—a kind of borrowed attraction—and that is sufficient : the child has been caught
in a wheel-work, as it were, and the first step has been
accomplished. The following is another example from
B. Perez.* "A child six years old, habitually very
inattentive, went to the piano one day, of its own ac-
cord, to repeat an air that pleased its mother; and it
remained there for over an hour. The same child, at
the age of seven, seeing its brother engaged about some
of his holiday-duties, entered and seated itself in its
father's study. 'What are you doing?' asked the
nurse, astonished at finding the child there. 'I am
doing a page of German ; it is not very amusing ; but
I wish to give Mamma a pleasant surprise.'" Here we
have another case of the genesis of voluntary attention, this time grafted upon a sympathetic, and not

* B. Perez : *L'Enfant de trois à sept ans,* p. 108.

upon a purely selfish feeling as in the former example. The piano and the German lesson did not spontaneously evoke attention; they awaken and maintain it through the medium of a borrowed force.

In every instance of the origination of voluntary attention this mechanism is invariably found to be the same,—but in endless variations, resulting in success, half-success, or failure : ever grasping natural motives, diverting them from their direct purpose, using them, if possible, as means for another end. Art bends nature to its purposes, and for this reason I call this form of attention, artificial.

Without assuming to enumerate all the different motives that artifice puts into play, in order to call forth and to consolidate voluntary attention, that is,— to repeat once more my former statement,—in order to impart to the purpose in view a power of action that it naturally does not possess, I shall now indicate three periods in point of time into which voluntary attention falls.

In the first period, the educator acts only upon simple feelings. He employs fear in all its forms, egotistic tendencies, the attraction of rewards, tender and sympathetic emotions, as well as our innate curiosity, which seems to be the appetite of intelligence, and which to a certain degree—no matter how weak— is found in everybody.

During the second period, artificial attention is aroused and maintained by means of feelings of secondary formation, such as love of self, emulation, ambition, interest in a practical line, duty, etc.

The third period is that of organization ; attention is aroused and sustained by habit. The pupil in the class-room, the workman in his shop, the clerk at his

office, the tradesman behind his counter, all would, as
a rule, prefer to be somewhere else ; but egotism, ambition, and interest have created by repetition a fixed
and lasting habit. Acquired attention has thus become
a second nature, and the artificial process is complete.
The mere fact of being placed in a certain attitude,
amidst certain surroundings, brings with it all the
rest ; attention is produced and sustained less through
present causes than through an accumulation of prior
causes ; habitual motives having acquired the force of
natural motives.   Individuals refractory to education
and discipline, never attain to this third period ; in
such people voluntary attention is seldom produced,
or only intermittently, and cannot become a habit.

It is unnecessary to show in detail that also in animals the transition from spontaneous attention to voluntary attention is similarly effected under the influence of education, and of training ; but here the
educator only has at his disposal limited means of
action, very simple in character.   He acts upon the
animal through fear, privation of food, violence, kind-
ness, caresses, and in this manner he succeeds in
making the animal contract certain habits, and through
artifice become attentive.   Among animals, as among
men, there are teachable and refractory individuals.
"A man," says Darwin,* "who trains monkeys to act
in plays, used to purchase common kinds from the
Zoölogical Society, at the price of £5 for each ; but
he offered to give double the price, if he might keep
three or four of them for a few days in order to select
one.   When asked how he could possibly learn so
soon whether a particular monkey would turn out a
good actor, he answered that it all depended on their

* " Descent of Man," Vol. I

power of attention.   If, when he was talking and ex-
plaining anything to a monkey its attention was easily
distracted, as by a fly on the-wall, or other trifling object, the case was hopeless.   If he tried by punishment to make an inattentive monkey act, it turned
sulky.   On the other hand, a monkey which carefully
attended to him could always be trained."

Accordingly, at the root of attention we find only
emotional states, attractive or repulsive tendencies.   In
the spontaneous form these are the only causes.   In
the voluntary form, it is the same ; yet with this difference, that here the feelings are of a nature more
complex and of slow formation, derived through experience from primitive tendencies.   If, while voluntary attention is still in its period of genesis, before it
has been organized and fixed by habit, you take away
from the school-boy all love of self, all emulation, all
fear of punishment, leave a fortune to the tradesman
or the workman, grant a competence to the clerk
from the very outset of his career, all their attention to their distasteful employments will at once be
scattered to the wind, for there is nothing left to
evoke and sustain it.   I confess that this genesis of
attention is very intricate; but it is conformable to
facts.   According to most psychologists it would seem,
that voluntary attention—which, although only a de-
rivative and acquired form, is yet the only one that
they regard—enters without an antecedent foundation.   "Voluntary attention is subject to the superior
authority of the Ego.   I give or withdraw it, as I
please ; by alternate turns I direct it toward different
points.   I concentrate it upon each point, as long as
my will can sustain its effort."*   If this be not a purely

* *Dict. scient. phil., 2e édit., Art. "Attention."*

conventional and fanciful description, if the author de-rives it from his own personal experience, I should not withhold my genuine admiration. But in truth, we should be destitute of all genius of observation, or blinded by prejudice, if we did not perceive that voluntary attention, in its durable form, is really a difficult state to sustain, and that actually many do not attain to it.

But if, as we have attempted to show, the higher form of attention is the work of the education that we have received from our parents, teachers, and surround-ings, as well as the education which later we have our-selves acquired in imitating that which we earlier ex-perienced, this explanation, nevertheless, only forces the difficulty further back ; for our teachers have only acted upon us, as others had previously acted upon them, and so on back through the generations. This, accordingly, does not explain the primordial genesis of voluntary attention.

How then does voluntary attention originate ? It originates of necessity, under the pressure of need, and with the progress of intelligence. *It is an instrument that has been perfected—a product of civilization.* The same progressive movement that in the order of moral events has caused the individual to pass from the control of instincts to that of interest and duty ; in the social order, from primitive savagery to the state of organization ; in the political order, from almost ab-solute individualism to the constitution of a govern-ment : this same onward movement, in the intellectual world, has also effected the transition from sponta-neous attention to the dominance of voluntary atten-tion. The latter is both effect and cause of civilization.

In the preceding chapter it was pointed out that,

in the state of nature the power of spontaneous attention, both for animals and men, is a factor of the foremost order in the struggle for life. In the course of
man's development from the savage state, so soon as
(through whatever actual causes, such as lack of game,
density of population, sterility of soil, or more warlike
neighboring tribes) there was only left the alternative
of perishing or of accommodating oneself to more complex conditions of life,—in other words, to go to work,—
voluntary attention also became a foremost factor in
this new form of the struggle for existence. So soon
as man had become capable of devoting himself to any
task that possessed no immediate attraction, but accepted as only means of livelihood, voluntary attention
put in an appearance in the world. It originated, accordingly, under the pressure of necessity, and of the
education imparted by things external.

It is easily shown that before civilization voluntary
attention did not exist, or appeared only by flashes
and then of short duration. The laziness of savages
is well-known ; travelers and ethnologists are all agreed
on this point, and the proofs and instances are so
numerous that it would be idle to quote authorities.
The savage has a passion for hunting, war, and gambling ; for the unforeseen, the unknown, and the haz-
ardous in all its forms ; but sustained effort he ignores
or contemns. Love of work is a sentiment of purely
secondary formation, that goes hand in hand with
civilization. And we may note, now, that work is the
concrete, the most manifest form of attention.

Continuous work is repugnant even to half-civilized
tribes. Darwin asked certain Gauchos who were
addicted to drink, gambling, and theft, why they did
not work. One of them answered : "The days are

too long."* "The life of the primitive man," says Herbert Spencer,† "is passed mainly in the pursuit of beasts, birds, and fish, which yields him a gratifying excitement; but though to the civilized man the chase gives gratification, this is neither so persistent nor so general. . . . . Conversely, the power of continued application, which in the primitive man is very small, has among ourselves become considerable. It is true that most are coerced into industry by necessity, but there are sprinkled throughout society men to whom active occupation is a need—men who are restless when away from business and miserable when they eventually give it up ; men to whom this or that line of investigation is so attractive that they devote themselves to it day after day, year after year, hardly giving themselves the rest necessary for health."

But, as in order to live at all, even as savages, it is necessary from time to time to perform some kind of drudgery, such labor, as is well known, usually devolves upon women, who, while their husbands sleep, work from fear of being beaten. It is accordingly possible—although at first it may seem a paradox—that voluntary attention first originated in woman.

Even among nations enjoying the advantages of long centuries of civilization, there exists a complete class of beings that are incapable of protracted work, —vagabonds, professional thieves, and prostitutes. The Italian criminologists of the new school, whether rightly or wrongly, look upon these as cases of atavism. The majority of civilized nations, however, have sufficiently adapted themselves to the exigencies of social life ; and they all are to a certain degree capable of

---

* *Voyage d'un Naturaliste au Tour du Globe*, p. 167.
† "Data of Ethics," Chap. X.

voluntary attention. But the number of those, of whom Spencer speaks, to whom voluntary attention is an urgent necessity—is very small indeed; and few and far between are those who profess and practice the *stantem oportet mori*. Voluntary attention is a sociological phenomenon. When we consider it as such, we shall better understand both its genesis and its infirmity.

The fact, we may say, has now been established, that voluntary attention is an adaptation to the conditions of a higher social life; that it is a discipline and a habit, an imitation of natural attention, which latter serves, at the same time, as its point of departure and point of support.

II.

Up to this point we have only examined, in our investigation of the mechanism of attention, the external impulsion arising from stimuli and surroundings which causes it to pass from one form to an other. We now come upon a much more obscure question, namely, the study of the internal mechanism through which a state of consciousness is laboriously maintained, in the face of the psychological struggle for life which incessantly tends to make it disappear. The relative monoideism we have had to deal with, which consists in the preponderance of a certain number of internal states, adjusted towards the same purpose and excluding all others, needs, in the case of spontaneous attention, no explanation. There a state (or a group of states) predominates in the consciousness, because it happens to be by far the stronger; and it is by far the stronger, because, as we have seen, all the tendencies of the individual conspire in its favor. The very contrary happens in the case of voluntary attention, especially in its highest artificial forms. What, accordingly, is the mechanism by which this state is maintained?

It is not requisite to investigate how the state of voluntary attention is produced in daily life. Like every other state of consciousness, it arises at the bidding of circumstances. But the feature that distinguishes it from other states, is, that it is prolonged and maintained. If a school-boy with but little taste for mathematics, recollects that he has a certain problem to solve, this is a simple state of consciousness; but if he sets about the task and persists, it is a state of voluntary attention. In order to leave no ambiguity concerning this point, I repeat that the whole problem consists in this very power of inhibition, of retention.

But how can we produce an arrested condition of this sort, an inhibition? We enter, with this query, upon a question but little known in physiology, and almost unexplored in psychology. Experience constantly proves, that in many cases we have the power to inhibit the movements of various parts of our body. But how is the equivalent of this inhibition produced in the mental order of things? If the physiological mechanism of inhibition were better known, we should probably be able to answer with more clearness. We accordingly ask the reader to regard the following remarks as an attempt replete with faults and omissions.

The fundamental property of the nervous system consists in the transformation of a primitive excitation into a movement. This is reflex action, the type of nervous activity. But we also know, that certain

excitations may impede, slacken, or suppress a movement. The best known, and oldest-studied, case is
that of the suspension of the movements of the heart
through irritation of the pneumogastric nerve. Since
the discovery of this fact, made by the brothers Weber
in 1845, physiologists have devoted much attention to
the study of cases in which the excitation of a nerve
prevents a movement or a secretion. Pflüger has
shown, that the splanchnic nerve has an inhibitory
action upon the small intestine. Since that date it
has moreover been established, that the movements of
the stomach and of the entire intestinal canal are similarly subject to inhibition. Cl. Bernard has referred
to the same cause the action of the vaso-dilator
nerves. Finally, this power of inhibition belongs not
only to the marrow and to the bulb ; it also exists in
the brain. Setschenof at first maintained that the
· central brain (*optic thalamus*) exerts an inhibitory influence upon the lower parts of the cerebro-spinal
axis. Many authors in recent times have referred the
phenomena of hypnotism to a cortical inhibition. Finally, according to Brown-Séquard, "inhibition is a
power possessed by almost all parts of the central nervous system and a considerable portion of the peripheral nervous system."

To explain this " negative reflex," different theories
have been invented, which it would be useless to
set forth here.* Let us note, however, that in his
" Functions of the Brain," Ferrier was the first who
referred attention to an action of the moderatory centres which he places in the frontal lobes. The recol-

---

* For the history of this problem down to the year 1879, see Hermann,
Handbuch der Physiologie, Vol. II, part. IJ, p. 33, et seqq. For the more recent
theories, S. Lourie, *I fatti e le teorie dell'inibizione*, in 8vo. Milano, 1888

lection of an idea, he says, depends on the motor element that enters into its composition. Attention depends on the restriction of the movement : there is repression of the external diffusion, and augmentation of the internal diffusion. The excitation of the motor centres, protected against external diffusion, expends its force internally ; repressed excitation of a motor centre occurs. Ferrier's reasons for localizing the moderatory centres in the frontal lobes, are as follows: Intelligence is proportionate to the development of attention ; and it is also proportionate to the development of the frontal lobes. Irritation of these lobes does not provoke any motory manifestation ; they are, accordingly, directive agencies, and expend their energy in producing changes in the centres of actual motor execution. Removal of them does not induce motor paralysis, but merely mental degeneration, resulting in loss of attention. The frontal lobes are imperfectly developed in idiots, whose power of attention is very weak. The frontal regions in animals become by degrees weaker, in proportion as the level of intelligence descends. We may add, that injuries to the frontal lobes will greatly lessen and frequently quite destroy the power of control.* The author declares, that "as to the physiological basis of this faculty of control, theoretical views only can be entertained."

Although the theory, that phenomena of inhibition take place in special organs, has become almost classical ; still, in recent times, several authors, basing their assertion upon experimental grounds, have maintained

* For the facts we may refer the reader to our own work, *Maladies de la Volonté*, p. 30, et seqq. Quite recently an American neurologist, Alex. Starr, in 23 cases of lesion of the frontal lobes, found in one half of his patients the following mental troubles : loss of the faculty of control, change of character, incapacity of fixing attention. "Brain," Jan. 1886, p. 570.

that "motor actions and actions of inhibition have their seat in the same elements."* "Every time a nerve is excited," says M. Beaunis, "there are produced in the nerve two kinds of modifications in opposite directions. If it be a motor nerve, there will be set up in the nerve an activity, revealed by a twitching of the muscle ; but beside this phenomenon, which is the most apparent and the one most studied, there is also produced a contrary state, which will tend to impede the shock, or to prevent its appearance. Thus, *at the same time,* in this nerve, there will be motor action and inhibitory action." † The motor process puts in an appearance sooner than the inhibitory process, and lasts a shorter time. The first excitation causes a maximum shock; but with the second excitation the inhibitory action, tending to be produced, diminishes its amplitude. In one of Wundt's experiments, "when a nerve is excited by a constant current, there is produced at the anode an inhibitory wave, which is recognized by the lessened excitability of the nerve, and which is slowly propagated from both sides of the anode : simultaneously, there is produced at the cathode a wave of excitation, that, with still greater swiftness and intensity, is propagated along from both sides of the cathode. An excited nerve, accordingly, is traversed at the same time by a wave of inhibition, and by a wave of excitation, and its excitability is but the algebraic resultant of these two contrary actions."

On this hypothesis, then, every excitation would

---

* Wundt, *Untersuchungen zur Mechanik der Nerven und Nervencentren,* 1871, 1876, and *Physiologische Psychologie,* Vol. I, Chap. IV. Beaunis, *Recherches expérimentales sur les conditions de l'activité cérébrale et sur la physiologie du nerf.* Paris, 1884. M. Beaunis has dwelt, more than any other physiologist, upon the importance for psychology of inhibitory actions.

† Op. Cit., p. 97.

determine in the nervous substance two modifications, the one positive and the other negative : a tendency to activity on the one side, and a tendency to the inhibition of this activity on the other side ; the final effect is nothing more than the resultant of these contrary actions, so that at one time impulsion and at another stoppage will prevail.

We have now very succinctly set forth nearly all that physiology teaches us concerning the mechanism of inhibition, and we shall have occasion to make use of it. We may revert now to the psychological phase of the problem.

The power of voluntary inhibition, whatever may be its *modus operandi*, is a secondary formation. It appears relatively late, as do all manifestations of a higher order. Volition in its positive, impulsive form— the volition which accomplishes something—is the first in order of time. Volition in its negative form, which hinders something, appears later ; according to Preyer,* toward the tenth month, in the very humble form of inhibition of natural evacuations.

But how is inhibition accomplished? This question cannot be answered satisfactorily. However, let us observe, that in this regard our position is exactly the same as when we are confronted with the opposite question : How do we produce a movement? In positive volition, the "I will" is usually followed by a movement ; that is to say, there is a setting into activity, in the brain, of motory images or appropriate motory residua ; a transmission of the nervous influx through the corona radiata to the corpora striata, to the inferior stratum of the cerebral peduncle, to the bulb, and then after decussation to the spinal marrow,

* "The Soul of the Child."

to the nerves, and finally to the muscles. In negative volition, the "I will" is usually followed by an inhibition.
Here the anatomical and physiological conditions of the
transmission are less accurately known ; upon the previously expounded hypothesis they would not be different from the preceding case.   But in both cases
consciousness directly knows only two things : the fact
of departure, and the fact of arrival ; the "I will" and
the act produced or inhibited.   All the intermediate
states escape it, and consciousness only knows them
through knowledge acquired, and indirectly.   Thus
situated as regards the sum of our present knowledge,
we must limit ourselves to stating, as a matter of fact,
that just as we possess the power of beginning, continuing, and increasing a movement, we also are able
to suppress, to interrupt, and to diminish any movement.

These general considerations bring us, at least,
to one positive result ; namely, that every act of volition, whether impulsive or inhibitory, *"acts only upon
muscles and through muscles".;* that any other conception is vague, incomprehensible, and chimerical; that
consequently, if, as we maintain, the mechanism of
attention is motory, then in all cases of attention there
must necessarily be a play of muscular elements, real
or nascent movements, upon which the power of inhibition acts.   We exercise no action (impellent or inhibitory) upon any other than voluntary muscles ; such
is our only and positive conception of will.   Of two
things, accordingly, one at least must be hit upon :
either to find muscular elements in all manifestations
of voluntary attention, or else to abandon all explanation of its mechanism, and to limit ourselves to saying that it exists.

Attention voluntarily addresses itself to perceptions, images, and ideals; or to speak more precisely, and to avoid all metaphor, the state of monoideism can be voluntarily maintained by a group of perceptions, images, or ideas, adapted to a purpose fixed upon in advance. In these three cases we have to determine the motor elements that are met with.

1. As regards perceptions, there are no difficulties. All our organs of perception are at the same time sensorial and motor. To perceive with our eyes, ears, hands, feet, tongue, nostrils, movements are needed. The more mobile the parts of our body, the more exquisite is their sensibility; the less perfect their motile power, the more obtuse their sensibility. Nor is this all; without motor elements, perception is impossible. We will call to mind a previous statement that if the eye be kept fixed upon a given object without moving, perception after a while grows dim, and then disappears. Rest the tips of the fingers upon a table without pressing, and the contact at the end of a few minutes will no longer be felt. But a motion of the eye, or of the finger, be it ever so light, will re-arouse perception. Consciousness is only possible through change: change is not possible save through movement. It would be easy to expatiate at great length upon this subject; for although the facts are very manifest and of common experience, psychology has nevertheless so neglected the rôle sustained by movements, that it actually forgot at last that they are the fundamental condition of cognition in that they are the instrument of the fundamental law of consciousness, which is relativity, change. Enough has now been said to warrant the unconditional statement, that where there is no movement there is no perception.

The rôle of movement in sensorial attention is not subject to the slightest doubt. The watch-maker who is minutely studying the wheel-work of a watch, adapts his eyes, hands, and body ; all other movements are suppressed. In laboratory experiments, instituted to study voluntary attention, this state of concentration through inhibition of movements, frequently attains an extraordinary height; we shall speak of it further on. But we may refer again to Galton's observations, reported in the preceding chapter, upon movements produced in a fatigued audience.

Attention, accordingly, means concentration and inhibition of movements. Distraction means diffusion of movements.

Voluntary attention, thus, may also act upon the expression of emotions ; as where we have strong motives for not outwardly betraying a feeling and possess a power of inhibition capable of preventing such expression. But it only acts upon muscles—upon muscles alone. Everything else escapes its control.

So far we have treated the problem from the point easiest of approach. We now come to that purely internal form, called "*reflexion.*" Images and ideas constitute its subject matter. In these two groups of psychic states, accordingly, we must now find the motory elements.

2. "It does not seem plain, at first," wrote Bain, as early as the year 1855, "that the retention of an idea, an image, in the mind is the work of our voluntary muscles. What are the movements produced, when I conceive to myself a circle, or think of St. Paul's? We can answer this question only by supposing that the mental image occupies in the brain and the other parts of the nervous system the same

place as the original sensation.   As there is a muscular element in our sensations, particularly in those of the highest order—in touch, sight, and hearing—this element must, in some way or other, find its place in ideal sensation—in recollection."   Since the time that this passage was written, the question of the nature of images has been closely and profitably studied, and solved exactly as therein indicated.*   Whereas, to the earlier psychologists, an image or idea was a kind of phantom, without definite seat, existing "within the soul," differing from perception not in degree but in nature, resembling it " at most only as a portrait resembles its original ;" to physiological psychology, on the contrary, there is between perception and image identity of nature, identity of seat, and only a difference of degree.   The image is not a photograph but a revival of the sensorial and motory elements that have built up the perception.   In proportion as its intensity increases, it approaches more and more to the condition of its origination, and so tends to become an hallucination.

Keeping closely to the motor elements of images (being the only ones that interest us), it is clear, that since there is no perception without movements, the latter, after they have been produced, leave behind in the brain motory residua (motory images, motory intuitions), exactly as the impressions upon the retina or skin leave behind sensorial impressions.   If the motory apparatus did not possess a memory of its own, images, or residua, no movement could be learned and made habitual.   Everything would always have

* Consult Taine, *De l'Intelligence*, Vol. II ; Galton, " Inquiry into Human Faculty," etc., pp. 83–114 ; Charcot, *Leçons sur les maladies du système nerveux*, Vol. III ; Binet, *Psychologie du raisonnement*, Chap. II ; Ballet, *Le Langage intérieur et les diverses formes de l'aphasie.*

to begin over again. However, it is not necessary to
fortify this by argument. Innumerable experiments
prove that movement is inherent in the image and
contained in it. Chevreul's famous experiment with
the pendulum may be regarded as typical. Is it necessary to cite more ? how there are people who plunge
head foremost into yawning chasms, through fear of
falling into them ? people who cut themselves with
razors, through the very fear of cutting themselves?
or the case of "thought-reading," which is but a reading of muscular states? and so many other facts that
are reputed extraordinary simply because people are
ignorant of the elementary psychological fact, that
every image contains a tendency towards motion ?
Of course, the motor element does not always possess
these enormous proportions, but it exists at least in a
nascent state ; just as the sensorial image does not always possess hallucinatory vividness, but exists simply
in outline in the consciousness.

3. If it is easy enough to establish the existence
of motor elements in images, the question of general
ideas or concepts, on the other hand, is more difficult.
Physiological psychology, it must be acknowledged,
has greatly neglected ideology, and the latter study is
in great need of revision from the standpoint of acquired experimental data. The study of perceptions
and images has paved the way for this task. But it
is not my intention to treat incidentally so great a
question. My purpose merely is, as a means of finding our true bearings, to group general ideas into the
following three great categories :

a) Those which result from the fusion of "similar"
images, without the aid of words ;

b) Those which result from the fusion of "dis-similar" images, with the aid of words ;

c) Those which are reduced to words; to language, accompanied with a vaguely represented outline, or even without any concomitant representation whatsoever.

I shall disregard the regulative concepts (those of time, space, and cause), the investigation of which would carry us too far from our path. And we may now examine, whether each of these three categories includes motor elements, upon which attention may act.

a) The first category comprises general ideas of the rudest sort, those which are met with in higher animals, children, and deaf-mutes, before the use of analytical language. The operation of the mind is limited to grasping very striking resemblances, and so to framing *generic images*— a term that really would be more correct than general ideas. The operation in question seems closely analogous to the process by which Galton, through superposing several photographs, obtains the composite portrait of a family, or an accumulation of resemblances with elimination of minor differences. But to maintain, as it has been maintained, that this process explains the formation of general ideas, is an untenable position. It explains only the very lowest grades ; being an operation that can deal only with gross resemblances. Now, do these generic images include a motor element? It is very difficult to say, and, in any case, it is to no purpose; for it is not at this stadium of mental life that voluntary reflection enters.

b) The second category comprises the majority of the general ideas that serve the current purposes of thought. In a more complete study of the present

subject, we would have occasion to establish an ascending gradation of groups, rising from the less general to the more general—a gradation indicating the
power of discerning ever fainter resemblances and
fewer and fewer analogies. All the degrees of this
ascending progression are met with in the history
of humanity. Thus it is that the Fuegians possess no
abstract terms. The American Indians have words to
designate the white oak, and the black oak ; but they
have no word for oak in general. The Tasmanians
have a term for each species of trees, but none for tree
in general ; and more naturally so, none for plant,
animal, color, etc.* Not to dwell upon these different
phases however, what is there in our mind when we
think these general ideas ? In the first place, a word,
which is the fixed element ; along with it an image,
less and less complex, less and less clear, in proportion as we ascend in generalization. This image is
an " *ex*tract," an *ab*stract. It is formed by a process
that the mind employs even to represent to itself an
individual image. Thus, it is observed, that the
representation I have of Peter, of Paul, of my dog, or
of any concrete being or object well known to me, can
only be an extract, an abstract, of the multiple perceptions that I have already had of it and which have
revealed the object to me under its different aspects. In
the representation of an individual image there is a
struggle among the former images of the same object
for supremacy in consciousness. In the conception of a
general idea, there is also a struggle among different
generic images, for supremacy in consciousness. An
abstract of the second or third degree is produced.

* Lubbock, "The Origin of Civilization," Ch. IX. Taylor, "Primitive
Culture," Vol. 1, Ch. VII.

There is thus formed a common nucleus, around which oscillate vague and obscure elements. My general conception of man or dog, if it persist ever so short a time in consciousness, tends to take a concrete form ; it becomes a white man or a black man, a spaniel or a bulldog. The motor element is especially represented by the word; we shall revert to this subject again. As to the images or abstracts of images annexed to the word, it would be difficult to tell what remains in them of the movements included in the original perceptions.

c) In the preceding category, in proportion as ideas grow more general, the part played by images gradually vanishes, the word more and more preponderates, up to the moment when it alone remains. We have, accordingly, the following progression, *viz.:* generic images without words, generic images with words, words without images. At this last stage we find purely scientific concepts. . But, does the word exist alone in the mind at this supreme point of abstraction ? I maintain, unhesitatingly, that it does. I cannot enter into details, which would carry me too far from my subject. I shall limit myself to observing, that if in fact there is nothing beneath the word, there is, there must be, a potential knowledge, the possibility of a cognition. ''In actual thought,'' says Leibnitz, ''we are accustomed to neglect the explanation of signs through that which they signify, knowing or believing that we have this explanation at our command ; in fact, we do not deem this application or explication of the words to be actually necessary. This method of reasoning I designate blind or symbolical. We employ it in algebra, in arithmetic, in fact, universally.'' Learning how to count in the case of chil dren, and, better still, in the case of savages, clearly shows, how the word, at first firmly clinging to objects, then to images, progressively detaches itself from them, to live an independent life of its own. Finally, the word much resembles paper-money (bank-notes, cheques, etc.), having the same usefulness and the same dangers. In the instance we are now considering, the motor element can be found only in the word. Recent researches, to which we have already referred, show that words do not exist in the same form in all individuals. To some it consists chiefly in articulative conditions. Stricker, in his book upon "Word and Music," has described from his own experience a perfect type of this: such are emphatically motory in nature. To others, words mainly consist in auditory images; this is the *inward word*, as it has been admirably described by V. Egger. Still others, far less frequently met with, think by the help of words *read* or *written.** The latter are visual.

Now, in the majority of men, these different elements act in unequal proportions. But everywhere and always, the word pronounced aloud, the purely internal sign, rests upon some, original form of perception, and consequently contains motor elements. It is unquestionably true, that the motor elements contained in general ideas of whatever category, are often very weak. This accords, moreover, with the fact of daily experience, that abstract reflection is impossible to many persons, and difficult and fatiguing to almost everybody.

We have dwelt at length upon this division of our

*There has been published a curious instance of the latter in the *Revue Philosophique*, January, 1885, p. 119. Also see Ballet, in the work cited above, Chap. III.

subject, because it is the least investigated, the most difficult, and most exposed to criticism.* But the reader will say : " We admit that there are motor elements in perceptions, images, and, to a less degree, in concepts. Still, that does not establish the fact, that attention acts upon them, and through them, and that it is a motory mechanism." True, upon this point we can cite no observation or experiment that would be decisive. The crucial test would consist in

* The study of a large number of normal and morbid cases has led to the knowledge of several types : motory, auditory, and visual, according to the group of images predominating in each individual; not to mention the ordinary or indifferent type. The person who thinks his words by articulating them, without hearing them (Stricker); and the person who thinks his words by hearing them, without articulation (V. Egger) ; the person who thinks his words by seeing them written, without either hearing or articulating them : all these represent irreducible types. This precludes all discussion. Each person is right, in so far as he himself, and people like him are concerned ; but he will be wrong, if he generalizes without restriction

It is much to be desired, that the work accomplished in the study of images and different forms of language, were likewise attempted for general ideas. It is probable, that here also we should find irreducible types. Thus Berkeley seems to me to think general ideas in the *visual* form. Any one who attentively reads certain passages (too long to transcribe here) of his famous Introduction to his " Treatise on Human Nature, " any one who studies it, not as a theory of general ideas, but as an instrument of psychological evidence, a kind of psychological confession, will conclude, that to Berkeley the general idea was a vision. " The idea of man, that I am able to form for myself," says he, " must be that of a white, black, or sunburnt man, straight or bent, tall, small, or of medium size. I am unable by any effort of thought to conceive the abstract idea before described " [namely, of color that is neither red, blue, green, nor etc., and which would still be a color]. On the other hand, the nominalists seem to me to think general ideas under the purely *auditory* form. The famous theory which makes of universals mere *"flatus vocis,"* (Roscelin, Hobbes, etc.,) appears, in my opinion, to admit of two interpretations. Taken literally, the theory is nonsense. The pure *"flatus vocis"* is a word in a language wholly unknown—a word not associated with any idea, and consequently a mere sound, a noise. It is hardly probable that sensible thinkers have ever maintained this theory in the form usually attributed to them. Their position, I think, may be explained by the fact, that the nominalists are of a hard, algebraic turn of mind, to whom the word is sufficient, without the awakening of any image ; in them there is no other representation than that of the sound. We are here very far from Berkeley.

Stricker, who is purely motory in this regard, who is unable to think a word without articulating it, who depends as little upon hearing, as is possible, expresses himself as follows : " I have to attach some sort of an object to every discovering whether a man, deprived of all external and internal motility—and of that alone—would be still capable of attention. But that experiment is not practicable. Even in the morbid cases that we shall study later on, there is nothing that approaches it. Let us incidentally remark, however, that it is impossible to reflect when running at full speed, even when we run without any other motive than the sake of running; or while climbing up a steep ascent, even where there is no danger and when we are not looking at the landscape. A multitude of instances prove, that there is an antagonism between great expenditure of movement and the state of attention. It is true, people reflect while striding about, and while fiercely gesticulating; yet here the object in view is rather one of invention than of concentration, and excess of nervous force is being discharged through various exits. Definitively, then, it is plain, that attention is an inhibition; and this inhibition cannot be produced save through a physiological mechanism which, in sensorial attention, prevents the expenditure of actual movements, and in reflection, the expenditure of movements in a nascent state : for the production of movement is restitution in the outward direction, a vanishing of the state of con-

word I possess, so that it will not appear to me like a dead term—like a word in a language that is unknown to me. When words occur to my mind such as 'immortality,' 'virtue,' and the like, I usually explain the same to myself not through words, but through visual images. At the word 'virtue,' for example, I think of a female form ; at the word 'bravery' of an armed man, etc.," (Op. cit., pp. 80, 81). This conception of abstract and general ideas might be called the antipode of nominalism. In medicine, it is said, that there are no diseases, but only patients ; in the same manner there are no general ideas, but only minds that think them in a different manner. Instead of proceeding philosophically, that is, seeking to reduce everything to unity, it were high time, it seems, to proceed psychologically, that is, to determine the principal types. A great many discussions in this manner would doubtless die a natural death. At all events, this task appears to me worthy of the trouble of being attempted.

sciousness—the nerve-force that produces it having transformed itself into motor impulsion. "Thought," says Setschenof, "is a reflex action reduced to its two first thirds"; or as Bain more elegantly expresses it : "To think is to refrain from speaking or acting."

To conclude, let us see what must be understood by the current expression "voluntarily to direct one's attention to any given object," and what takes place in such a case.

"What is accomplished in such cases," says Maudsley very aptly,* "is the excitation of certain nervous currents of ideas, and their maintenance in action until they have called into consciousness, by radiation of energy, all their related ideas, or as many of them as it may be possible, in the then condition of the brain, to stimulate into action. It would appear, then, that the force that we mean by attention is rather a *vis a fronte* attracting consciousness, than a *vis a tergo* driving it. Consciousness is the result, not the cause, of the excitation. The psychological mode of expression puts the cart before the horse; the problem in reflection is not, as it is said, to *direct* consciousness or to *direct* the attention to an idea, but to *arouse* consciousness of it by stirring it up to a certain pitch of activity."

However, a doubtful point still remains. If we admit that the general mechanism of attention is motory and, in the particular case of voluntary attention, that it chiefly consists of an action of inhibition, we are still induced to ask, how is this inhibition effected, and upon what does it act. This is a question fraught with so much obscurity, that we can do no more than limit ourselves to its simple enunciation;

* "Physiology of Mind," pp. 317, 318, 321.

and yet it will be better to attempt an answer, even though purely conjectural, than to appear to elude the difficulty.

It would perhaps not be altogether unprofitable to search for light in an analogous but more simple order of phenomena.

Reflex movements, whether reflex actions proper, natural and innate, or reflex actions that are acquired, secondary, and fixed by repetition and by habit, are produced without volition, hesitation, or effort, and may continue a long time without fatigue. They call into action, in the organism, only those elements necessary to their effectuation, while their adaptation to ends is perfect. In the strictly motory order of things, they are the equivalent of spontaneous attention, which, similarly, is an intellectual reflex action that presupposes neither choice nor hesitation nor effort, and may likewise continue a long time without fatigue.

But there are other classes of movements that are more complex and artificial ; as, for instance, writing, dancing, fencing, all bodily exercises and all mechanical handicrafts. In these instances, adaptation is no longer natural, but laboriously acquired. It demands the exercise of choice, repeated endeavor, effort, and at the outset is accompanied by fatigue. Daily observation shows, that at first a great number of useless movements are produced : thus a child learning to write, moves arms, eyes, head, and sometimes a part of its body. The end to be sought here is to prevent this diffusion, and by appropriate associations and disassociations to produce the maximum of useful work with the minimum of effort. The reason of the fact observed is, that isolated movements do not exist and that a muscle in contracting acts upon the adjacent muscles and often upon many others. Success is attained by some lucky hit, after repeated efforts : with apt people quickly ; with awkward persons slowly, or perhaps never at all. The mechanism, however, remains always the same ; it consists in firmly strengthening certain movements, in coördinating them into simultaneous groups or into series, and in suppressing, in *inhibiting* all others.

Voluntary or artificial attention proceeds in the same manner. When one prepares to enter into this laborious state, one sees states of consciousness arising by groups or by series—for isolated states of consciousness no more exist than isolated movements. Among them there are many that do not serve the principal aim, or deviate from it. Here, also, there are useless or detrimental states of consciousness that, if possible, must be suppressed. A considerable portion of our task consists just in this negative work, whereby the intrusive elements are expelled from consciousness, or reduced to their least intensity. But how is this accomplished ? Either we must abandon all explanation, or admit an action of inhibition exerted upon the motor elements of the states of consciousness involved. In such cases we have a very distinct feeling of sustained effort. And whence could that feeling come, if not from the energy expended to accomplish the acts of inhibition ? For, indeed, the ordinary course of thought, left to itself, is exempt from any such sensation. If it be objected that from this view-point the fundamental mechanism of voluntary attention remains hidden, it may be replied that indeed the fundamental mechanism of all volition remains hidden. In consciousness the two extremest termini alone enter, namely, the beginning and the end ; everything else takes place in the physiological domain, whether it be a question of doing or preventing, of producing a movement or effecting an inhibition.

Attention is a momentary, provisional state of the mind ; it is not a permanent endowment, like sensibility or memory. It is a form (the tendency to monoideism) imposed upon a subject-matter (the ordinary course of states of consciousness) ; its point of departure lies in the chance of circumstances (spontaneous atten- tion) or in the fixing in advance of a determinate aim (voluntary attention). In both cases, emotional states, tendencies, must be awakened. In this we have the primitive *direction* of attention. These lacking, all else miscarries; if they vacillate, attention will be un- stable ; if they do not continue, attention will vanish. A state of consciousness having thus once become preponderant, the mechanism of association enters into play in its multiple forms. The work of *" direction "* consists in choosing the appropriate states, and in maintaining them (by inhibition) within our conscious- ness, in order that in their turn they may fructify, and so onward through a series of selections, inhibi- tions, and consolidations. Attention can accomplish nothing more than this ; in itself it creates nothing, and if the brain be sterile, if the associations are poor, it will act its part in vain. Voluntarily to direct one's attention, is for many people an impossible task ; con- tingent, for all.

III.

Every one knows by experience that voluntary at- tention is always accompanied by a feeling of effort, which bears a direct proportion to the duration of the state and the difficulty of maintaining it. Whence does this feeling of effort come, and what does it mean ?

Effort from attention is· a particular instance of effort in general, the most common and best known manifestation of which is the effort that accompanies muscular work. Three opinions have been propounded to account for the origin of this feeling :

First, that it is of central origin—anterior to movement, or at least simultaneous therewith ; that it passes from within to without ; that it is centrifugal—efferent ; the feeling of energy being displayed ; not resulting, as in sensation proper, from an external influence transmitted by the centripetal nerves (Bain).

Secondly, that it is of peripheral origin—posterior to the movements produced ; that it passes from without to within ; that it is afferent ; the feeling of energy that *has been* displayed ; that, like every other sensation, it is transmitted through centripetal nerves from the periphery of the body to the brain (Charlton, Bastian, Ferrier, W. James, etc.).

And, thirdly, that it is both central and peripheral : a feeling of force exerted, or feeling of innervation, and also a feeling of movement accomplished ; that first it is centrifugal, and then centripetal (Wundt). This composite theory also seems to be that accepted by J. Müller, one of the first who studied this question.

The second thesis, which is the most recent, appears the most tenable one. It has been very carefully expounded by Mr. W. James in his monograph " *The Feeling of Effort*," (1880), in which the thesis of the feeling of energy developed prior to movement, has been criticized with great acumen. The author, in discussing the facts successively involved, has pointed out, that if in cases of paralysis of a part of the body or of an eye, although the member remains motionless, the patient have the feeling of energy developed (which seems to justify the thesis of a feeling of a central innervation anterior to movement), it is because a movement is really produced in the other part of the body, in the corresponding limb, or in the eye which has not been paralyzed. He concludes thence, that this feeling is a complex afferent state resulting from the contraction of muscles, the extension of the tendons, the ligaments, and the skin, from compressed articulations, from an immovable chest, closed glottis, knit eyebrows, set jaws, etc.; in a word, that, like all sensations, it is of peripheral origin. Even for those who can not accept this thesis as definitive, it is certain, that it explains the facts far more satisfactorily and far more in conformity to the general laws of physiology than the hypothesis which connects this feeling with the motor nervous discharge—the motor apparatus being insensible in the centripetal direction.

Let us examine, now, the particular case of effort accompanying attention. The earlier psychologists limited themselves to establishing its existence, but they do not explain it. They speak of it only in vague, mysterious terms, as of a *"state of the soul,"* and of a hyperorganic manifestation. They see in it "an action of the soul upon the brain, designed to set the latter into activity." Fechner, I believe, is the first (1860) who attempted a precise localization of the different forms of attention, by referring them to definite parts of the organism. The following passages of his I have deemed worthy of citation as an attempt at explanation :

"The feeling of the effort of attention in the various

organs of sense seems to me to be but a muscular feeling (*Muskelgefühl*) produced upon the setting into motion, by a kind of reflex action, the muscles that are connected with the different sensory organs.   The question then arises : With what muscular contraction can the feeling of effort in attention be connected when we strive to remember something?   My internal sense gives me a definite answer to this question.   I experience a very marked sensation of tension, not in the interior of the cranium, but a tension and a contraction as if of the skin of the head, and a pressure from without inward over the whole cranium, evidently caused by a contraction of the muscles of the skin of the head—circumstances which perfectly agree with such expressions as "to rack one's brains, one's head " (*sich den Kopf zerbrechen*), "to collect one's thoughts " (*den Kopf zusammennehmen*).   During an illness from which I once suffered, I was utterly unable to endure the slightest effort of continuous thought (and at the time in question I had not adopted any particular theory); during this illness the muscles of the skin, and particularly those of the occiput, got into a very marked degree of morbid sensibility, every time I attempted to reflect."

In the following passage Fechner describes this feeling of effort, first in sensorial attention and then in reflection :

"If we transfer our attention from the domain of one sense to that of another, we at once experience a definite feeling of change of direction—a feeling difficult to describe, but which any one can reproduce by experiment.   We designate this change as a tension differently localized.

"We feel a tension directed forward in the eyes,

directed sidewise in the ears, and varying with the degree of attention, according as we look attentively at, or listen attentively to anything. This is why we speak of the effort of attention. We very clearly feel the difference when we rapidly change the direction of attention from the eye to the ear. In the same manner the feeling is differently localized according as we wish to smell, taste, or to touch anything carefully.

" Whenever I wish to represent to myself as clearly as possible any recollection or image, I experience a feeling of tension very much like that of attentive vision or attentive audition. But this quite similar feeling is localized in a manner totally different. While, in the attentive vision of real objects as well as of successive images, the tension is felt in front, and while in bringing attention to bear upon the other sensorial regions, it is only the direction toward the external organs that changes, the rest of the head not giving any feeling of tension—on the contrary, in the case of recollection and of images, I become conscious that the tension withdraws completely from the external organs of the senses and seems rather to occupy the part of the head which the brain fills. If I wish, for example, vividly to represent to myself an object or a person, such object or person seem to be brought to me all the more vividly in proportion as I strain my attention not forward, but, as it were, backward." *

Since the time at which Fechner's work appeared, the researches, already mentioned, of Duchenne, of Darwin, and of the various authors that have studied the movements of expression, have imparted much greater precision and clearness to this subject. The

* *Elemente der Psychophysik*, Vol. II, pp. 490 and 475.

part sustained by the respiratory movements, of which Fechner does not speak, is also to be noted. The movements of respiration are of such great importance, that in certain cases they engender of themselves the feeling of effort. Ferrier has shown this by a very simple experiment. If one stretches out one's arm, and holds the index-finger in the position required to fire a shot from a pistol, one can experience even without actually moving his finger the feeling of energy developed. Here, then, is a clear case of the feeling of energy developed, without real contraction of the muscles of the hand, and without perceptible physical effort (which is Bain's thesis). "But, if the reader repeat the experiment and carefully give heed to the state of his respiration, he will observe, that his consciousness of effort coincides with a fixation of the muscles of the chest and that he closes his glottis and actively contracts his respiratory muscles in proportion to the sum of energy felt to be exerted by him. Let him place his finger as before and *continue to breathe* the whole time, and he will find, that however much he directs his attention towards his finger, he will not feel the slightest trace of consciousness of effort until the finger itself has been actually moved, and then it will be locally connected with the muscles that act. Only when this essential, ever present, respiratory factor has been set aside, as in the latter instance has been done, can consciousness of effort acquire any degree of plausibility in being attributed to the centrifugal current."

To sum up, muscular contractions are found everywhere and at all times. Even in cases in which we remain motionless, we will find, if we carefully observe, that intense reflection is accompanied by an incipient word, motions of the larynx, the tongue, and the lips. In people that do not belong to the motory type—such, consequently, as are most unfavorable to our thesis—there is a state of ideal audition, or of ideal vision : the eye, although closed, is fixed upon imaginary objects. Czermak, and after him Stricker, have pointed out, that if after having inwardly contemplated the image of an object supposed very near, we abruptly pass to the mental vision of a very distant object, we will feel a marked change in the state of innervation of the eyes. In real vision, in such a case as this, one must pass from the state of convergence to the state of parallelism of the visual axes, that is, one must innerve the motor muscles of the eye in a different manner. The same operation, though weaker and in a nascent stage, takes place in that internal vision which accompanies reflection. Finally, with all persons and in all cases, there are modifications in the rhythm of respiration.*

We can now answer the question above put, namely, What is the origin of the feeling of effort in attention, and what does it mean ?

It has its origin in the physical states now so often enumerated—the necessary conditions of attention. It

---

* M. Guge (of Amsterdam) has recently given the name of *aproseky* (from ἀ, not, and προσέχειν, to give attention) to the incapacity of fixing one's attention on a certain object by reason of a diminution of the nasal respiration due to certain circumstances, such as adenoid tumors in the pharyngo-nasal cavity, polyps of the nose, etc.—A child, seven years old, had succeeded in learning, during a whole year, only the three first letters of the alphabet. Having been operated upon for its adenoid tumor, the same child in a single week learned the entire alphabet. A number of college students, suffering from the same affection, were unable to learn anything. Their sensation was headache and vertigo every time they endeavored to fix their attention. They were able without fatigue to read a phrase six or ten times, but without understanding what they had read, though not thinking of anything else. This circumstance distinguishes this state from ordinary distraction. (*Biologisches Centralblatt*, January 1, 1888.)

is simply their reverberation in consciousness. It depends on the quantity and quality of the muscular contractions, of organic modifications, etc. Its starting-point is peripheral, like that of every other sensation.

This means, that attention is an abnormal, a transient state, producing a rapid exhaustion of the organism ; for after effort there is fatigue, and after fatigue there is functional inactivity.

One obscure point remains. When we pass from the ordinary state to the state of sensorial attention or reflection, an augmentation of work is produced. A man worn out by a long walk, by great mental exertion, or who succumbs to sleep at the end of the day's task ; a person recovering from a serious illness ; in a word, all debilitated individuals, are incapable of attention, because like every other form of work, it requires a reserve capital that may be expended. In passing from the state of distraction to the state of attention there is, accordingly, transformation of a condition of stress into *vis viva ;* of potential energy into kinetic energy. Now this forms an *initial* moment that is very different from the moment of effort felt, which is an effect. This observation is incidentally made ; I do not insist upon it. But the investigation of this question cannot be profitably attempted before we have surveyed our subject in its totality.

IV.

Experimental researches upon voluntary attention have confirmed, and imparted greater precision to, certain conclusions, which nevertheless follow naturally from a correct understanding of the subject. These researches are either direct or indirect, according as they investigate attention in itself, in its individual variations, in its normal and morbid states, or according as they study it as the means and instrument of other researches upon the duration of perceptions, associations, judgment, choice, etc. Attention is, in fact, the fundamental psychical condition of almost all psychometrical researches.*

Obersteiner, to whom attention is essentially a fact of inhibition, found that attention generally requires more time in ignorant individuals than in people of culture; in women than in men, which latter, by their particular mode of life, have developed the power of inhibition; in old people, than in adults and young people, which doubtless must depend on a less rapid functional activity.

A series of experiments, performed upon the same person, has given as the average time in the normal state, 133σ†; in case of headache, 171σ; in the state of fatigue and of somnolence, 183σ. In a patient at the beginning of general paralysis the average time was 166σ; at the second period of this malady when the condition of the patient just about allowed experimental investigation, 281σ has been attained, and even 755σ. On the other hand, Stanley Hall, who was fortunate enough to discover a subject that had the power of correctly reacting in the hypnotic state, has established a very considerable diminution of the

* Consult for details and arrangement of experiments: Obersteiner, " Experimental Researches on Attention," in *Brain*, Jan., 1879; Wundt, "Physiological Psychology," Vol. II, Chap. XVI; Exner in Hermann's "*Handbuch der Physiologie*," Vol. II, part II, p. 283, et seqq; Stanley Hall, "Reaction, Time, and Attention in the Hypnotic State," in *Mind*, April, 1883.

† σ, the unit in all the figures given, is equal to one one-thousandth of a second.

time of reaction, which passes from an average of 328σ (normal state) to 193σ (hypnotic state)—a result that might have been foreseen, by reason of the monoideism peculiar to the state of hypnosis.

Wundt and Exner have made other experiments upon persons in the normal condition. First, the subject is taken in the state of distraction ; the impression against which he is to react, coming upon him suddenly, and without having been described in advance. Then, the impression to be received by him is described as to its nature and its force, but not as to the time at which it is to be produced. Finally, the impression is accurately and completely set forth (both as to nature and time), a definite signal notifying the subject when the impression is to follow. In this upward progression from uncertainty toward certainty, the time of reaction constantly diminishes, as might have been anticipated. Thus, while in the case of distraction it may rise to the enormous figure of 500σ, it falls in the second case to 253σ, and with the signal to 76σ.

These experiments present to us in the simplest form the state called *expectant attention* or *pre*-attention. They further necessitate a few remarks, with a view to corroborating what has been previously stated.

If, in expectant attention, the *intellectual* aspect be considered, it will be seen that it is a preparatory stage in the course of which the image of an event foreseen or presumed, is evoked. The state of monoideism is formed ; with the result that the real event is but the reinforcement of the representation already existing. In some experiments two, almost simultaneous, impressions have been produced, and the question is to determine which is anterior in time. If they are of a different nature, the one auditive (the stroke of a bell), the other visual (an electric spark), there is a tendency to consider as anterior, first, either the stronger of the two impressions, or, secondly, that toward which our attention during the experiment was directed. While engaged in researches of this kind, Wundt was able, at will, and according to the direction given to his attention, to perceive first now the one and now the other. When the two excitations are of the same nature, only the first is distinctly noticed ; the second passes by unperceived.

If the *motor* aspect of expectant attention be considered, it will be found that this state induces a preparatory innervation of the nervous centres and the muscles, which is liable, at the least shock, to be converted into a real impulsion. Representation alone, in this manner, can produce a reaction, without external cause.

This explosive state is especially produced in cases in which the expected impression is not beforehand determined ; which might be called cases of expectant attention in general. The motor innervation is distributed throughout all the sensorial regions. There is produced a feeling of disquietude and discomfort ; of tension, such that a falling body or an accident attending the experiment will bring about an automatic reaction.

When the expected impression is determined beforehand, the path of motor innervation will be traced out in advance ; instead of being diffused, the tension is localized. The time of reaction can become zero and even attain a negative value.

When the reaction is to be effected through different processes, or as the result of different excitations, it is necessary that a change be produced in the cen-

tres that shall produce a change in the direction of the
nervous paths—a very fatiguing state. If one persists
in reacting, the time will increase enormously, and
reach, according to Exner, as high as a second.

We must also mention the experimental researches
of N. Lange upon the oscillations of sensorial attention. In the silence of the night, the ticking of a
watch, placed at a certain distance, is at one moment
not heard and in the next it is distinctly reinforced.
The same is true of the sound of a waterfall ; and similar oscillations have been observed with optic and
tactile sensations. These variations are not objective ;
they can only be subjective.   Must we—as is usually
done—ascribe them to fatigue of the sensory organs ?
Our author does not think so.   In his opinion they
come from a central cause, and are due to oscillations
of attention.   When one is attentive to two simultaneous excitations, one optic and the other acoustic, the
oscillations, if they are of peripheral origin, ought to
be independent of each other. Yet such is not the
case ; the two kinds of oscillations never coincide ;
they are always separated by a clearly defined interval.
What is the cause of this periodicity of the oscillations ? According to Lange it is to be sought in the
oscillation of the images that accompany sensorial
perception. The reinforcement that in this way exists in attention, is here owing to the fact, that to the
present impression is added the image of an anterior
impression. Sensorial attention would seem to be an
assimilation of the real impression that remains unchanged before us, with the anterior image, which undergoes oscillations.*

* Lange, *Beiträge zur Theorie der Sinnlichen Aufmerksamkeit und der*
Activen Apperception," in the *Philosophische Studien*, 1887. Vol. IV, Part III.

It will be seen, in fine, that attention in no respect resembles an independent activity ; that it is bound up with perfectly determined physical conditions, that it acts only through the latter, and is dependent on the same.

CHAPTER III.

THE MORBID STATES OF ATTENTION.

To COMPLETE the study of attention, an examination of the morbid cases still remains. I do not propose here to construct a pathology of attention : such a pretension were too ambitious, and the undertaking premature. But there are certain facts, neglected by psychology, which, although somewhat common-place, still demand review. Their importance for the better understanding of the mechanism of normal attention, will not escape the reader's notice.

Our daily speech usually contrasts with attention the state called " distraction "; but this state in our language (the French) has an equivocal sense. It designates certain states of the mind, apparently, very similar, yet at bottom totally contrary. We call " distracted " people whose intelligence is unable to fix itself with any degree of persistence, and who pass incessantly from one idea to another, at the mercy of their most transient whims, or of any trifling events in their surroundings. It is a perpetual state of mobility and dispersion, which is the very reverse of attention. It is frequently met with in children and in women. But the term "distraction " is also applied to cases entirely different from this. Thus there are people who, wholly absorbed by some idea, are also really " distracted " in regard to what takes place around them ; they afford no hold to external events, and allow the latter to flit by without penetrating their minds. Such people appear incapable of attention for the very reason that they are very attentive. Many scholars have been noted for their "distraction," and so well known are the instances that it is useless to cite them. While those whose distraction amounts to dispersion are characterized by the incessant transition from one idea to another, those whose distraction amounts to absorption are distinguished precisely by the impossibility or the great difficulty of a transfer of this kind. They are riveted to their idea, are willing prisoners without any desire to escape. Their condition, in fact, is a mitigated form of that morbid state which we shall study later on under the name of the "fixed idea."

Yet such manifestations, daily occurring, in fact all the different forms of "distraction," are, upon the whole, but little instructive, and we shall derive greater profit from dwelling upon forms that are clearly pathological. Without pretending to anything like a systematic classification of the latter, we shall endeavor to group them according to some rational order. To accomplish this purpose, normal attention must serve as our starting-point, and it devolves upon us only to note the variations of its nature and its deviations.

Certain authors, in studying the disorders of attention, have referred them to various, generally admitted types of mental disease, such as hypochondria, melancholy, mania, demency, etc. This method, besides entailing perpetual reiterations, has the still greater inconvenience of not placing the fact of attention in the proper fullness of light. Attention, in such cases, is studied, not for its own sake, but merely as a

symptom.   With us, on the contrary, it has to be regarded as a fact of the foremost order, while all the
rest is but accessory.   It is requisite that the morbid
forms be attached to the common trunk—the normal
state ; it is requisite, that at all times we should clearly
discern its proper relations.   On this condition alone
can pathology instruct us.

If, as we have formerly done, we now define attention as the *temporary* predominance of an intellectual
state, or of a group of states, accompanied by natural
or artificial adaptation of the individual ;—if this be
taken as its normal type, we shall be able clearly to
note the following deviations :

1. *Absolute* predominance of one state, or one
group of states, that becomes stable, fixed, and that
cannot be dislodged from our consciousness.   It is no
longer a simple antagonist of spontaneous association,
limiting its activity to direction of the latter ; no, it is
a destructive, tyrannical power, enslaving everything,
not allowing of the prolification of ideas save in one
direction, imprisoning the current of consciousness
within a narrow bed, from which it cannot escape, and
more or less sterilizing all that which is extraneous to
its own predominance.   Hypochondria, and, better still,
fixed ideas and ecstasy, are cases of this class.   They
form the first morbid group, which I shall designate
hypertrophy of attention.

2. In the second group I shall comprise cases in
which attention cannot be maintained, or in which
often, indeed, attention cannot form.   This incapacity
is produced under two main conditions.   At times
the current of ideas is so rapid and exuberant, that the
mind becomes a prey to an unbridled automatism.   In
this disorderly flux no particular state either lasts or

predominates ; no centre of attraction is formed, even for a moment. Here the mechanism of association retaliates ; it alone acts with all its power, and without opposition. Such are certain forms of delirium, and above all acute mania. At other times, when the mechanism of association does not pass beyond the average intensity, there is absence or diminution of the power of inhibition. Subjectively, this state manifests itself through the impossibility or extreme difficulty of effort. Convergence is impossible, either spontaneous or artificial ; all is unsteady, undecided, and dispersed. Numerous instances of this are met with in hysterical patients, in persons suffering from irritable weakness, in convalescents, in apathetic and insensible individuals, in intoxication, in extreme states of bodily and mental fatigue, etc. This impotency coincides, in short, with all forms of exhaustion. By way of contrast to the former, we shall designate this group *atrophy of attention.*

Incidentally we may remark that the first group of morbid states is allied rather to spontaneous attention, and the second to voluntary attention. The one marks an exaggerated force, the other an exaggerated weakness, of the power of concentration. The one is an evolution, and tends toward *increase* ; the other is a dissolution, tending towards *decrease.* Already, pathology verifies what has previously been stated. Voluntary attention, like all artificial products, is precarious, vacillating ; disease does not transform it, but causes it to collapse. Spontaneous attention, on the contrary, like all natural forces, may extend and amplify to the very verge of extravagance, but it can only be transformed ; at bottom, its nature does not alter : it is like a light breeze at first, that afterwards becomes a tempest.

3. The third group embraces, not the morbid forms of attention, but cases of congenital infirmity. Such are instances in which spontaneous attention, and all the more so, voluntary attention, do not form, or, at least, only appear intermittently. This, in different degrees, is met with in idiots, in imbeciles, in the weak-minded, and in the demented.

After this hasty classification, let us pass to details.

I.

It is well, in the first place, to observe, that there is an almost insensible transition from the normal state to the most extravagant forms of the fixed idea. Everybody must have experienced what it is to be haunted by a musical air, or some insignificant saying, that obstinately keeps coming back without any visible reason. This is the fixed idea in its lightest form. The state of preoccupation so called, takes us one degree higher : anxiety about a sick person, or that attending the preparation for an examination, a long journey to be undertaken, and a hundred other facts of this kind, which without constituting an actual beleaguerment of consciousness, do yet all act by way of repetition. Notwithstanding its intermittence, the idea remains vivid, suddenly starting up from the depths of unconsciousness. It has more stability than any other, and its momentary eclipses do not prevent it from playing the principal part. As a matter of fact, in every sound human being, there is always a dominant idea that regulates his conduct ; such as pleasure, money, ambition, or the soul's salvation. This fixed idea, which lasts throughout life—except in cases where another is substituted for it—becomes finally resolved into a fixed passion ; which once more proves that attention and all its forms of appearance depend on emotional states. The metamorphosis of attention into a fixed idea is much more clearly seen in great men. "What is a great life?" asks Alfred de Vigny; "A thought of our youth, realized in mature age." In many famous men this "thought" has frequently been so absorbing and tyrannical, that one can hardly dispute its morbid character.

This transformation of spontaneous attention into a fixed idea, a phase decidedly pathological, is very pronounced in hypochondriacs. Here, we are able to follow its evolution, and to note all its degrees; for this disease embraces a great many stages from the slightest preoccupation to the most complete obsession. Although it cannot germinate and grow but in a favorable soil, and although consequently it presupposes certain physical and mental conditions, yet it does not, in its origin, rise beyond the average level of spontaneous attention ; the augmentation is effected slowly, by degrees. And it makes no difference, in fact, whether the sufferings of the patient be real or imaginary : from the subjective, psychological point of view this is all one. We know, indeed, that the mere fact of fixing our attention upon any part of our body, the heart, the stomach, the intestines, etc., produces in consciousness strange sensations—an instance of the general law, that every state of vivid consciousness tends to actualize itself. Some people have, in this respect, peculiar gifts. Sir J. Brodie said, that he could feel pain in any region of his body whatever, by strongly fixing upon it his attention.   Now, to fix our attention simply means, to allow a certain state to persist and to predominate.   This predominance, at first harmless, increases through the very effects it produces. A centre of attraction is established, which little by little obtains supreme control of consciousness. It then grows to be a perpetual preoccupation, an incessant inspection of the state of each organ and the products of each function ; in short, the state of complete hypochondria makes its appearance as its picture so often has been portrayed.

But there are fixed ideas more extraordinary and more infrequent, which by virtue of their purely intellectual nature are, so to speak, the caricature of reflection.   These are fixed ideas properly so called. Various contemporary authors have studied them with much care.*   Unfortunately, the dissertations and collected results of observations upon this subject have not passed out of the domain of psychiatry, and hitherto psychology has profited little by them—at least as far as regards attention.

However, it seems almost universally agreed that fixed ideas may be classed into three great categories :

1. Simple fixed ideas of a purely intellectual nature, which are most frequently pent up in consciousness, or are not manifested outwardly save through certain insignificant acts ;

* Westphal, "Ueber Zwangsvorstellungen " (*Archiv für Psychiatrie,* 1878) ; Berger, " Grübelsucht und Zwangsvorstellungen" (*Ibid.,* Vol. VIII) ; Krafft-Ebing, "Lehrbuch der Psychiatrie," and "Ueber Geistesstörungen durch Zwangsvorstellungen" (*Zeitschrift für Psychiatrie,* Vol. XXXV) ; Griesinger, "Ueber einen wenig bekannten psychopathischen Zustand" (*Archiv für Psych.,* Vol. l) ; Meschede, "Ueber krankhafte Fragesucht" (*Zeit. für Psych.,* Vol. XXVII) ; Buccola, *Le idee fisse e le loro condizioni fisiopatologiche* (1880) : Tamburini, *Sulla pazzia del dubbio e sulle idee fisse ed impulsive* (1883) ; Luys, *Des Obsessions pathologiques* (Encéphale, 1883) ; Charcot & Magnan, *De l'onomatomanie* (in the *Archives de Neurologie,* 1885).

2. Fixed ideas accompanied by emotions, such as terror and agony, agoraphobia, the insanity of doubt, etc.;

3. Fixed ideas of an impulsive form, known by the name of irresistible tendencies, that manifest themselves in violent or criminal acts (theft, homicide, suicide).

Although there is no clear line of demarcation between the three classes, still, we may say, that the specific character of the first is a perturbation of the intelligence, that the second belongs rather to the emotional order, and that the third depends upon an enfeeblement of the will. The latter two will be rigorously excluded from our investigations, because they are parcel of the pathology of feelings and the will. It is by far preferable to keep strictly to cases that are free from all alloy—to cases strictly comparable with that state of relative monoideism which is called attention.

But even in restricting ourselves to this group, examples of fixed ideas will not be lacking. They have received different names according to their predominant character. With some the fixed idea assumes a mathematical form (arithmomania). Why are people of such and such a size ? Why are houses of such and such dimensions ? Why are trees of such or such a height ? And so on with every other object. Still more frequently, it consists in an endless necessity to count, to add, and to multiply. "A certain woman, affected with numerous symptoms of hysteria could not see a street without beginning at once, and against her will, to count the number of paving-stones ; then would follow an enumeration of all the streets of the town, then of all the towns of Italy, and finally of

Italy's streams and rivers. If she beheld a bag of corn, there immediately began in her brain the work of enumerating the number of grains of corn in the city, in the province, and in the whole country. . . . . She confessed, that not only did she feel impelled by an irresistible force to make these odd computations, but that moreover these fixed ideas of hers were so well organized, that if during her laborious task she chanced to be interrupted by the sheer impossibility of proceeding, or by any other cause, she would suffer from a feeling of agony accompanied by indescribable physical tortures."* I have myself been told of a certain young man who spends the greater part of his time in calculating the hours of departure and arrival, for each station, of all the railway-trains on the entire surface of the globe. He generously bestows railroads upon countries that have none, and regulates at will this imaginary traffic. He compiles very elaborate time-tables, covering enormous sheets of paper, draws curves, and establishes connections at the various junctions. He is, moreover, a very intelligent young man.

Another form of fixed idea consists in asking endless questions upon some abstract problem, which the patients themselves regard as insoluble. The Germans call it " *Grübelsucht,*" the English " metaphysical mania." The interrogatory form peculiar to it has moreover procured it the name of *Fragetrieb.* A certain man, in a case reported by Griesinger, no sooner heard the word " beautiful " uttered, than he began, in spite of every effort, to put to himself an inextricable and indefinite series of questions upon the most abstruse problems of æsthetics. The word "to be " precipi-

---

* Roncati in Buccola, work cited.

tated him into an endless metaphysical investigation. This patient, a highly cultivated man, tells us in his confession : "I am ruining my health by incessantly thinking of problems that reason will never be able to solve, and which despite my most energetic efforts of will, wear out, without a moment's respite, my strength. The procession of these ideas is incessant. . . . . This metaphysical reflection is too continuous to be natural. . . . . Every time that these ideas return I try to drive them away, and I seek to persuade myself to follow the natural course of thought, not to confuse my brain with such very obscure problems, and not to abandon myself to the meditation of things abstract and insoluble. And yet I am unable to escape from the continuous impulsion that keeps hammering at my mind, or from the unchanged, fixed tendency that pursues me, and does not leave me one moment of rest."*

I shall give a final instance of the fixed idea, as reported by Tamburni, on account of its purely intellectual character : "A young law-student, the son of neuropathic parents, was completely taken up with the idea of knowing the origin, the why and the how of the forced circulation of bank-notes. . . . . This thought kept his attention continually strained, prevented him from doing anything else, placed a bar between the external world and himself, and whatever efforts he might make to rid himself of it, he was utterly unable to accomplish that purpose. Finally concluding that notwithstanding his long reflections and far-going researches to the end of solving this vexed problem, he was in-

---

* Griesinger, Op. cit. To understand the true significance of this case, it is to be observed that the question here is that of a metaphysician in spite of himself.

capable of any other mental work, he fell into such a state of despondency and apathy that he desired to discontinue his course of studies. . . . . His sleep was insufficient and broken ; frequently he lay awake whole nights, ever absorbed by his dominant idea.   In this case a very singular phenomenon must be noted ; namely, that in consequence of the continuous tension of his mind upon the problem of bank-notes and their forced circulation, he at last retained permanently before his eyes the image and picture of the bank-notes themselves, in all their varieties of form, size, and color.   The idea, with its incessant repetitions and intensity, came to assume a force of projection that made it equivalent to reality. Yet he himself had ever the full consciousness that the images floating before his eyes were merely a freak of his imagination."   A careful medical treatment, and some very clear explanations imparted by a professor, finally helped to improve his condition.   "The veil that enveloped his mind, though rent asunder so far as regards bank-notes of large denominations, still persisted in regard to those of smaller value, the images of fifty centime notes, still continuing to appear to him."   At last all his troubles disappeared.

Sometimes the fixed idea consists in an inroad of names that must be found again—names of indifferent people or unknown persons (onomatomania) ;—but the feeling of intense anxiety by which it is usually accompanied, relegates it by preference to our second category.

It will perhaps be said : " These people and their like are simply insane."   They certainly are not of sound mind ; but the epithet insane is undeserved. They are debilitated, unbalanced.   Their frail, unstable mental coördination yields to the slightest shock ; but it is a loss of equilibrium, not a fall. The authors that have investigated the determining causes of fixed ideas, all reach the same conclusion ; they find it, namely, to be a symptom of degeneration. One might even maintain, that not everybody who may wish it can have fixed ideas. A primordial condition—the neuropathic constitution—is requisite. The latter may be inherited, or it may be acquired. Persons of the one class are the offspring of parents to whom they are indebted for the sad legacy of degenerate organisms. These are by far the most numerous. The others have been exhausted by circumstances and mode of life : physical or intellectual fatigue, emotions, strong passions, sexual or other excesses, anæmia, debilitating diseases, etc.* Finally, by both roads the same result is reached. And so the fixed idea, even in its simplest form—that which now concerns us and which appears entirely theoretical and as if confined to the field of purely intellectual operations—is nevertheless not a purely internal phenomenon, without physical concomitants. Quite the contrary. The organic symptoms by which it is accompanied indicate neurasthenia : symptoms such as headaches, neuralgia, feeling of oppression, perturbation of motility, of the vaso-motors, or the sexual functions, insomnia, etc. The psychic phenomenon of the fixed idea is but the effect, among many, of one and the same cause. Still, it is to be observed, that if to the physician it suffices to refer all these multiple manifestations to one single source, *viz.*, degeneration, to the psychologist, however, there remains a much more difficult task. Be-

*For a detailed exposition of the causes conf., particularly, Tamburini, Op. cit., p. 27.

sides the general cause he should discover the *par-* *ticular* causes of each case. Why, for example, does such and such a form prevail with such and such an individual ? Why does this exclusive preoccupation take the form of calculation in one, of names in another, and of bank-notes in still another? What are the secondary causes that here have given the malady such and such a direction? Each case should be studied separately. Upon the supposition that the investigation might accomplish the purpose set, it were the best course to begin with the worst and most serious cases—the very ones that we have decided not to consider. These, as a matter of fact, are the simpler, and some of them being connected with a known organic apparatus (as, for instance, the fixed idea of certain erotomaniacs) we would thus have a point to start from and would find ourselves in the possession of a clue. But we should court certain failure if at the very outset we were to apply psychological analysis to the intellectual forms of the fixed idea. However, it is not incumbent upon us here to attempt this work. Our sole purpose, at present, is, to examine more closely the mechanism of the fixed idea, to discover in what respect it resembles the mechanism of attention and in what respect it differs from it.

And to this proposition we may at once answer, that between the two there is no difference of kind but only a difference of degree. The fixed idea has greater intensity, and, above all, a longer duration. Take a given state of spontaneous attention ; suppose that through artificial means we are able to strengthen and, particularly, are able to render it permanent. The metamorphosis into a fixed idea would then be complete ; the whole array of irrational conceptions

that form its retinue and present a fictitious appearance of insanity being of necessity added to it as the
mere result of the logical mechanism of the mind.
The term "fixed idea" designates the principal part
of the complete psychological state ; yet only a part—
the centre, namely, whence all departs, and whither
everything reverts. The permanence of a single
image, a single idea, and nothing more, would con-
flict with the conditions of the existence of consciousness, which requires change. *Absolute* monoideism,
if such there exist, is, at the utmost, met with in the
extremest forms of ecstasy, as will be explained further
on. The mechanism of the fixed idea consists in associations of states of consciousness in a single direction—associations that at times are loose and of little
coherency, yet more frequently held together by a
compact, logical bond which expresses itself in incessant interrogations.

Certain authors, Westphal particularly, in noting
the differences between fixed ideas and mental disorders designated as insanity, have made the important remark, that "the fixed idea is a formal alteration of the process of ideation, but not of its content ";
in other words, there is alteration, not in the nature,
the quality of the idea, which is normal, but in its
quantity, intensity, degree. To reflect upon the origin
of things, or upon the usefulness of bank-notes, in itself is a perfectly rational act, and this state is in no
wise comparable with that of a beggar who believes
himself a millionaire, or of a man who thinks himself
to be a woman. The "formal" perturbation consists
in the inexorable necessity that compels the association always to follow one and the same path. Since
intermissions and momentary changes of direction oc-

cur, these patients, who are gifted with a high degree of intelligence, and more than ordinary culture, possess a full consciousness of the absurdity of their condition : the fixed idea appears to them as a foreign body that has taken up its abode in their system and which they are unable to dislodge; yet, withal, it is not able to take entire possession of them ; it remains "a miscarried, delirious idea."

This *formal* character of the fixed idea well shows its close relationship to attention. The latter, as we have often said, is but a mental attitude. Perceptions, images, ideas, and emotions are its content-matter ; attention does not create them, it simply isolates, strengthens, and illuminates them ; it is a mode merely of their appearance. Even current speech itself establishes a distinction between the ordinary form and the attentive form of the states of the mind.

I am, accordingly, fully inclined to hold, with Buccola, "that the fixed idea is attention at its highest degree—the extreme limit of its power of inhibition." There is no boundary-line, even of fluctuation, between the two ; and to recapitulate, if we compare them with each other, the following is what we obtain :

1. In both cases we find predominance and intensity of a state of consciousness, but greatly superior in the case of the fixed idea. The latter, in consequence of organic conditions, is permanent, it lasts: it has the disposal of a psychical factor of great importance—time.

2. In both cases the mechanism of association is limited. In attention this exceptional state does not last long ; consciousness reverts spontaneously to its normal condition, which is the struggle for existence between heterogenous states. The fixed idea prevents all diffusion.

3. The fixed idea presupposes—and this is one of the ordinary effects of degeneration—a considerable weakening of the ˉwill, that is, of the power to react. There is no antagonistic state that is able to overthrow it. Effort is impossible or vain. And hence the state of agony of the patient, who is conscious of his own impotency.

Physiologically regarded, the condition attending the fixed idea may probably be represented in the following manner. In its normal state the entire brain works: diffused activity is the rule. Discharges take place from one group of cells into another, which is the objective equivalent of the perpetual alterations of consciousness. In the morbid state only a few nervous elements are active, or, at least, their state of tension is not transmitted to other groups. It is not necessary, let it be remarked, that the nervous elements in question should occupy a single point or limited region of the brain; they may be sprinkled here and there, provided they be closely joined and associated together for the common work. But whatever may be their position in the cerebral organ, they are as a matter of fact isolated; all disposable energy has been accumulated in them, and they do not communicate it to other groups; whence their supreme dominance and exaggerated activity. There is a lack of physiological equilibrium, due probably to the state of nutrition of the cerebral centres.

Esquirol called the fixed idea a catalepsy of the intelligence. It might also be compared to a phenomenon of the motor order—contracture. Contracture is a prolonged constriction of the muscles; it results from an excess of irritability of the nervous centres and the will has not the power to destroy it. The

fixed idea has a similar cause ; it consists in an excessive tension, and the will has no power over it.

II.

The fixed idea might be termed the chronic form
of hypertrophy of attention ; ecstasy being its acute
form.   It is not our purpose here to investigate ex-
haustively this extraordinary state of the mind.   We
have treated it elsewhere,* in its negative aspect, as
annihilation of will.   At present we are to consider it
from its positive side, as exaltation of intellect.

The comparison of attention and ecstasy is not
novel ; the analogy between the two states being so
great that various authors have actually employed attention to define ecstasy.   " It is," says Bérard, "a
vivid exaltation of certain ideas, which so absorb attention, that sensations are suspended, voluntary motions
arrested, and vital action itself frequently slackened."
Michéa defines it as "a deep contemplation with abolition of sensibility and suspension of the locomotive
faculty."   A. Maury expresses himself even more ex-
plicitly, saying : " A simple difference of degree sepa-
rates ecstasy from the action of forcibly fixing an idea
in the mind.   Contemplation implies exercise of will,
and the power of interrupting the extreme tension of
the mind.   In ecstasy, which is contemplation carried
to its highest pitch, the will, although in the strictest
sense able to provoke the state, is nevertheless unable
to suspend it."†

As in the fixed idea, so between the normal state

* *Les Maladies de la volonté*, Chap. V.
† Maury, *Le Sommeil et les Rêves*, p. 235.

and ecstasy, intermediate degrees are distinguishable. Men endowed with great power of attention, can isolate themselves at will from the external world. Inaccessible to sensations and even to pain, they temporarily live in that particular state which has been called *contemplation.* The oft-quoted story of Archimedes at the capture of Syracuse, whether true or not as fact, is certainly psychologically true. The biographies of Newton, Pascal, Walter Scott, Gauss, and many others, have furnished numerous examples of this intellectual rapture.

" Before the invention of chloroform, patients would sometimes endure painful operations without betraying any symptom of pain, and afterwards would declare, that they had felt nothing, having by a powerful effort of attention concentrated their thoughts upon some subject, by which they had been completely entranced.

" Many martyrs have endured torture with perfect serenity, which, according to their own confession, they experienced no difficulty in maintaining up to the last. Their entranced attention was to such a degree absorbed by the beatific visions that were presented to their enraptured eyes that bodily tortures did not give them any pain." *

Political fanaticism has more than once produced the same effects. But everywhere and always some great passion has served as the basis of support; still further proving, that vivid and stable forms of attention depend on emotional life and on that only.

Passing by the intermediate degrees, in order to come to ecstasy proper, and neglecting all the other physical and psychical manifestations that accompany

* Carpenter, " Mental Physiology," Chap. III,

this extraordinary state, let us consider exclusively a single fact, namely, extreme intellectual activity accompanied by intense concentration upon a single idea. This is a state of intense and circumscribed ideation; all life is gathered up, as it were, in the thinking brain, in which a single representation absorbs everything else. Still, the state of ecstasy, although in every individual it may exalt the intelligence to its highest degree of power, is nevertheless unable to transform it. It cannot act in the same manner upon a narrow and ignorant mind as upon a broad and highly-cultivated one. From the view-point of our present subject we may, accordingly, distinguish two categories of mystics. With the first class the internal event consists of the apparition of some dominant *image*, around which all else revolves (as the Passion, the Nativity, the Virgin, etc.), and which is expressed by a regular series of movements and speeches, as those of Marie de Mærl, Louise Lateau, and the entrancements of Voray. In the second category—the grand mystics—the mind, after having traversed the region of images, reaches the domain of pure *ideas*, and there remains fixed. Further on, I shall attempt to show that this higher form of ecstasy may at times reach the state of complete, absolute monoideism, that is, the state of perfect unity of consciousness, which consists in a single state without any change whatever.

In order to trace this ascending progression toward absolute unity of consciousness, of which even the most concentrated attention is but a very faint outline, we need not have recourse to probable hypotheses, nor need we proceed theoretically and a priori. I find in the "*Castillo interior*" of Saint Theresa a description, step by step, of this progressive concentration of consciousness, which starting from the ordinary state of diffusion, assumes the form of attention, passes beyond the latter, and by degrees, in a few rare cases, attains to perfect unity of intuition. The illustration in question is exceptional and single, but in the present matter one good observation is better than a hundred second-rate ones.* The observation deserves, moreover, our fullest confidence. It is a confession made at the behest of the spiritual power, the work of a very delicate mind, and a very able observer that well knew how to wield language to express the finest shades of thought. Furthermore, I must request the reader, not to allow himself to be led astray by the mystic phraseology in which the observation is couched, and not to forget, that here, a Spanish woman of the sixteenth century analyzes her mind in the language and ideas of her time ; we shall be able, however, to translate the same into the language of contemporaneous psychology. This task I shall now attempt, endeavoring at the same time to point out the ever increasing concentration and incessant narrowing of consciousness that we have noted, as they are described from her own personal experience.

There exists, says she, a castle built of a solitary diamond of matchless beauty and incomparable purity ; to enter and to dwell in that castle is the supreme aim of the mystic. This castle is within us, within our soul ; we have not to step out of ourselves, to penetrate its recesses ; though, nevertheless, the road thereto is long and difficult. To reach it, we have to pass through seven stations : we enter the castle through the seven

* It is highly probable, that one would find more of the same kind, by examining the mystic literature of different countries. The passages here quoted are from the "Interior Castle," and a few from the "Autobiography."

degrees of "prayer." In the preparatory stage we are still immersed in bewildering varieties of impressions and images—occupied with "the life of the world"; or, as I should prefer to translate it, consciousness still follows its usual and normal course.

The first objective point, or stage, is reached through "oral prayer." Which, interpreted, means, that praying aloud, articulate speech in other words, produces the first degree of concentration, leading the dispersed consciousness into a single, confined channel.

The second stage is that of "mental prayer," which means, that the inwardness of thought increases; internal language is substituted for external language. The work of concentration becomes easier: consciousness, to prevent aberration, no longer requires the material support of articulate or audible words; consciousness is now satisfied with a series of uncertain images unfolding before it.

The "prayer of recollection" (*oraison de recueillement*) marks the third stage. What this means, I must confess, slightly puzzles me. In this state I can only perceive a still higher form of the second period, separated from it by a very subtle shade, and appreciable only to the mystic consciousness.

Up to this point there has been activity, movement, and effort. All our faculties are still in play; now, however, it becomes necessary "no longer to think much, but to love much." In other words, consciousness is about to pass from the discursive form to the intuitive form, from plurality to unity; it tends no longer toward being a radiation around a fixed point, but a single state of enormous intensity. And this transition is not the effect of a capricious, arbitrary will, nor of the mere movement of thought left to it-

self ; it needs the impulsion of a powerful love, the
"touch of divine grace," that is, the unconscious co-
operation of the whole being.

The "prayer of quietude" brings us to the fourth
station ; there "the soul no longer produces, but receives" ; this is a state of high contemplation, not exclusively known to religious mystics alone.   It is truth
appearing suddenly in its totality, imposing itself as
such, without the long, slow process of logical demon-
stration.

The fifth station, or "prayer of union," is the beginning of ecstasy ; but it is unstable. It is "the
meeting with the divine betrothed," but without lasting possession.   "The flowers have but half-opened
their calyxes, they have only shed their first perfumes."
The fixity of consciousness is not as yet complete, it
is still liable to oscillations and deviations ; as yet it
is unable to maintain itself in this extraordinary, un-
natural state.

Finally it attains to ecstasy in the sixth degree,
through "the prayer of rapture."   "The body grows
cold ; speech and respiration are suspended, the eyes
close ; the slightest motion may cause the greatest
efforts. . . . .   The senses and faculties remain without. . . . .   Although usually one does not lose all
feeling (consciousness), still *it has happened to me to
be entirely deprived of it ;* this has seldom come to
pass, and has lasted but for a short time.   Most frequently, feeling is preserved, but one experiences an
indefinable sort of agitation, and although one ceases
to act outwardly, one does not fail to hear.   It is like
some confused sound, coming from afar.   Still, *even
this manner of hearing ceases when the entrancement is
at its highest point.*"

What, then, is the seventh and last station that is reached by "the flight of the spirit"?   What is there beyond ecstasy?   Union with God.   This is accomplished "suddenly and violently . . . . but with such force that we should strive in vain to resist the impetuous onset."   God has now descended into the substance of the soul, and becomes one with it.   This distinction of the two degrees of ecstasy, is not, in my opinion, without reason.   At its highest degree, the very abolition of consciousness is attained by its excess of unity.   This interpretation will appear well-grounded, upon reference to the two passages above italicized, *viz.*: " It has happened to me to be entirely deprived of feeling ", and "this manner of hearing ceases when the entrancement is at its highest point." We might cite other passages to this effect from the same author.   It is remarkable, that in one of her "great raptures" the Divinity appeared to her entirely without form, as a perfectly empty abstraction. Such, at least, appears to be the gist of her own words : " And so I say, that the Divinity is like a transparent diamond, supremely limpid, and much larger than the world."*   In this I can discern nothing else than a simple rhetorical comparison, a literary metaphor.   It is, indeed, the expression of complete unity of intuition.

This piece of psychological evidence has enabled us, as we have seen, to follow consciousness, step by step, to its furthermost degree of concentration, to *absolute* monoideism.   It enables us, moreover, to answer a question, frequently raised, yet which has only theoretically been settled ; namely, Can a state of uniform consciousness subsist ?   The testimony of certain mys-

* Autobiography, p 126.

tics apparently justifies an answer in the affirmative. To be sure, it is a settled and common truism, that consciousness only exists through change ; at least it has been admitted since the time of Hobbes : "*Idem sentire semper, et non sentire, ad idem recidunt.*" .But this law has been infringed in the case of a few exceptional individuals, in very rare instances and during very short spaces of time. In ordinary ecstasy consciousness attains to its maximum of constriction and intensity, but it still preserves the discursive form : it differs only in degree from very strong attention. The greatest mystics alone have attained, by a still stronger effort, to absolute monoideism. They all, in every country, in all times, and without knowledge of each other, have regarded perfect unity of consciousness, the ἕνωσις, as the supreme and rarely attained consummation of ecstasy. Only four times in his life did Plotinus obtain this favor, according to Porphyrius, who himself obtained it but once, at the age of sixty-six years.* Consciousness, at this extreme point, cannot long endure—they declare. But this instability, which they explain in their own way as due to their unworthiness of such beatitude and the impossibility of a finite mortal becoming infinite, is in reality explainable from psychological and physiological causes. Consciousness is placed without its necessary conditions of existence, and the nervous elements that are the supports and agents of this prodigious activity cannot long bear the intense strain. The individual then falls back to earth again, and again becomes "the little donkey a-browsing away his mortal existence."

* Porphyrius, "Life of Plotinus," Chap. XII.

III.

The debilitation of attention is extreme in mania, which, as is known, consists of a general and permanent over-excitation of the psychic life. The diffusion is not internal only; it is also being incessantly transferred outwards, and is being expended at each instant. A constant agitation is manifested, a continual need to speak, to shout, and to act violently. The state of consciousness is immediately projected outwards. "Maniacs," says Griesinger, "are often able, for a considerable length of time, to keep up an expenditure of muscular force to which the strength of a sane individual would not be adequate. They are seen to spend weeks, or whole months almost, without sleep, a prey to violent fury, and the only explanation of this enormous muscular expenditure seems to be, that through an anomalous condition of the sensibility of the muscles these patients are destitute of the feeling of fatigue." At the same time, sensations, images, ideas, feelings follow each other with such astonishing rapidity that they scarcely attain to the condition of complete consciousness, and so that frequently the bond of association uniting them is totally undiscoverable to the spectator. Or in the very words of one of these maniacs, "It is really frightful to think of the extreme rapidity with which ideas succeed one another in the mind." To recapitulate, we find here, in the mental order of things, a disordered flow of images and ideas; in the motory order, a flux of words. shouts, gesticulations, and impetuous movements.

We need not further pursue this subject and show that in mania all conditions that are contrary to the state of attention are combined. Neither concentration nor adaptation nor duration are at all possible. It is the triumph supreme-of cerebral automatism, left entirely to itself, and free from all control. With maniacs, moreover, there prevails at times an extreme exaltation of memory; they are able to recite long poems, forgotten years before.

In this intellectual chaos no particular state can last any length of time. "But let us bring some powerful action to bear upon the mind of a maniac, or let some unforeseen event arrest his attention, and all of a sudden you will find him rational, and his reason will last as long as the impression has sufficient power to retain his attention.".* Here again we have an instance that teaches us upon what causes spontaneous attention depends.

Under the general head of exhaustion we include a very numerous group of states, in which attention cannot pass beyond a very weak stage. Here it has not to struggle, as in mania, against an excessive automatism; its weakness is its own. Examples are found in hysterical persons, in persons afflicted with melancholy, in the first stages of intoxication, at the approach of sleep, and in extreme physical or mental fatigue. Children affected with St. Vitus's dance are also but little capable of attention.

These morbid or semi-morbid states confirm the position we took in our investigation of the normal state, *viz.*, that the mechanism of attention is essentially motory. In exhaustion it is impossible, or extremely difficult to fix the attention; and this—to repeat a former statement—implies, that here an intellectual state cannot predominate, nor last, nor pro-

* Esquirol, *Maladies Mentales*, Vol. II, p. 47.

duce an adequate adaptation.   This cerebral exhaustion, which results from some defect or other of nutrition, manifests itself in two ways : in the first place, by a state of consciousness without intensity and without duration, and in the second place by an insufficiency of motor nervous influx.   Now, if the movements which, as it is termed, "accompany" attention, movements of respiration, of circulation, of the head, the limbs, etc., are weak and without vigor ; if these motor phenomena, as we maintain, are not concomitants, but elements, integral parts, of attention, that impart to the intellectual state a delimitation, a support, and, as it were, a body ; and finally, if in the normal state their effect is to strengthen the sensation, the image, or idea through an action of resilience : in such case it is clear, that all these conditions are here absent or defective, and that in exhaustion there can only be produced attempts at attention, feeble and without duration.   This, in fact, is what occurs.

Let us take the case of intoxication, the simplest and the most commonplace of all, and which moreover presents this advantage, that here the dissolution of the movements can be followed to the end.   It is a well-known biological law, that dissolution follows the inverse order of evolution ; that its work of destruction proceeds from the complex to the simple, from the less automatic to the more automatic.   This law is verified in the case of intoxication.   At first our most delicate movements become unsettled, the movements of utterance, which grow embarrassed, the movements of the fingers, which lose their precision ; later, the semi-automatic movements, that constitute walking : the body reels ; still later the intoxicated person is unable even to keep his seat, he falls to the ground ; finally follows the total loss of reflex motions, the man is "dead"-drunk ; in extreme cases, loss even of respiratory movements. We shall disregard the last phases of the dissolution of movements, which are purely physiological ; and reverting to the beginning, let us see what takes place in consciousness. Is a man after drinking really capable of attention, and above all, of reflection? The state of exaltation, which is then produced in some men, is the very reverse of the state of concentration. The power of inhibition weakens ; men abandon themselves totally to the verification of the dictum, "*In vino veritas.*" Then, little by little, consciousness becomes obscured ; the states it assumes float indistinctly about, without clear outlines, phantom-like. The debilitation of attention and that of movements, accordingly, go hand in hand ; they are but two aspects of what at bottom is really a single phenomenon.

However, there now arises another question ; we do not wish to treat it by way of episode, and shall, accordingly, merely point it out to the reader. If the state of nervous exhaustion prevents attention, we are brought through this fact to the source of attention. The healthy man is capable of attention, effort, and work in the widest sense ; the man whose strength is debilitated, is incapable of attention, effort, or work. But work performed is not the result of nothing ; it does not fall from the skies ; it can only be the transformation of pre-existing energy—the change of stored, potential, energy into actual, kinetic, energy. This potential energy stored in the nervous substance, is itself the effect of chemical actions taking place within it. Such, accordingly, would be the ultimate condition of attention.   For the present, I shall confine myself to this simple observation.*

According to the theory generally accepted, sleep also is the consequence of exhaustion, and perhaps of a kind of intoxication.   The few authors who have studied attention during sleep, start from the implicit or explicit hypothesis, that attention is a power, a faculty, and they have put to themselves the question whether during sleep that faculty is suspended. From our point of view, the problem is differently presented. We proceed to inquire whether the *state* of relative monoideism, which we denominate attention, is or is not constituted during dream-activity.

It is certain, that often a sensation or an image becomes predominant in the series of states of consciousness that during dreams flit through the mind in rapid and disorderly succession.   An instant of inhibition then occurs ; we have the feeling even of adaptation, of adjustment—at least partially and temporarily so ; and finally, this predominant state is always accompanied by some strong affection or emotion (fear, anger, love, curiosity, etc.)—with the result that we find therein all the essential characteristics of spontaneous attention.'

But are the equivalent elements of voluntary, of artificial, attention discoverable in that state ?   In the first place, we have to discard entirely a certain class of cases that naturally we would feel tempted to cite as affirmative instances.   Such cases are the solutions of problems, scientific discoveries, artistic or mechanical inventions, clever combinations, that have been revealed in dreams. Tartini, Condorcet, Voltaire, Franklin, Burdach, Coleridge, and many others, have

*See Conclusion, § 2.

reported personal observations so well known that mere reference thereto is here sufficient. All these phenomena are the product of cerebral automatism, a species of activity that is directly antagonistic to voluntary attention. In dreams, people only discover, invent, and find solutions, in strict accordance with their habits and cast of mind. Coleridge composes a poem, but he does not solve algebraical problems ; Tartini completes his sonata, but he does not evolve a financial combination. These results are the long work of antecedent incubation, at times conscious, but oftener unconscious (that is, purely cerebral), which all of a sudden attains its ultimate state of maturity. The condition of the mind during dreams is thus as unfavorable as can be to the formation of voluntary attention : on the one hand we find rapidity and incoherence of associations ; on the other disappearance or extreme impairment of all coördination. The highest, most delicate, and most complex forms are the first to disappear. And yet the will-power is not always suspended, for sometimes we strive to maintain ourselves in a state that pleases us, or endeavor to escape from an unpleasant situation. Cases also occur that present an outline at least of voluntary attention ; which is natural enough with those who have contracted the habit. At times, the absurdity of our dreams is revolting, and we endeavor to make clear to ourselves their contradictions. At times, we make computations, the inexactitude of which is mortifying, and we try hard to discover the causes of error.* But these are exceptions. If sleep were not the suspension of effort in one of its most laborious forms, it would not fulfill its office of reparation.

* See several instances in Sully, " Illusion," Chap. VII.

As regards natural somnambulism, and still more so as regards hypnotism, the question is still far from having been cleared up.   Braid, who was the first to divest provoked somnambulism of the vesture of the marvelous in which it was enveloped, reduced the whole psychology of this phenomenon to a " concentration of attention " : a view, which with only slight modifications has been maintained by Carpenter, Heidenhain, Schneider, and especially by Beard (of New York).   The last psychologist takes it to be " a functional perturbation of the nervous system, the activity of which is concentrated within a limited region of the brain, the rest remaining inactive and thus producing loss of volition."   According to his favorite comparison, the cortex of the brain resembles a chandelier with numerous gas-burners.   When all the jets are lighted, we have the waking state ; when all are turned down low, almost to the point of extinguishment, we have sleep ; when all have been extinguished with the exception of a single one, still brightly burning and consuming all the gas, we have hypnosis in its different stages.   This theory of " concentrated attention " has been subjected to much criticism* and hardly seems applicable to all cases. Could hypnotism as produced in chickens and crabs by Kirchner, Czermak, and Preyer, possibly be attributed to an abnormal concentration of attention ? It is certain, indeed, that the hypnotized individual is well prepared for the state of monoideism ; but is this state, artificially produced by suggestion, really comparable to attention proper ?   Does it not rather resemble the fixed idea ?

* Conf. Stanley Hall in *Mind*, April, 1885, and Gurney, *Ibid.*, Oct., 1884.

IV.

Idiocy has various degrees, from complete nullity of intelligence to simple weak-mindedness, according to the point at which arrest of development has taken place. Some imbeciles even have a particular talent for the mechanical arts, for drawing, for music, or arithmetic, which is all the more salient from its being surrounded by complete vacuity. These isolated faculties have been compared to the instincts of animals.

Here the most elementary conditions of attention are lacking, or only appear by intermittent flashes. The defective senses deliver only dull impressions, and the higher centres are unfit to elaborate them and bring them together. The condition of the *motor* faculty, that essential factor of attention, also deserves to be noticed. It is continually presenting anomalies —paralysis, convulsions, contractures, epilepsy ; or a kind of restricted automatism, which incessantly repeats the same movements, such as continually swaying the body to the accompaniment of a monotonous chant, beating the walls, opening and shutting without end the same piece of furniture, etc. In all this there is no power of coördination or of control. "Imbeciles and idiots," says Esquirol, "are bereft of the faculty of attention, which renders them incapable of education,—a fact that has repeatedly been the subject of my personal observation. Wishing to obtain plaster-casts of a large number of insane individuals, I was successful with maniacs, even the most furious of them, and with patients affected with melancholy ; but I could not get the imbeciles to keep their eyes closed long enough for the plaster to take form, no

matter how willing they had been to have the operation performed.   I have even seen them cry because
the cast could not be successfully taken, and repeatedly endeavor to maintain the position in which they
had been placed, but always in vain ; they were unable to keep their eyes closed for more than one or
two minutes."*   The lowest grades of idiots and imbeciles do not even possess the spontaneous attention
that animals enjoy with a view to the preservation of
life.   The less refractory specimens are, to a slight
degree, amenable to education. Séguin and others
have, by patient training, obtained some favorable
results.   Without inquiring whether the great efforts
made with this end in view since half a century have
had any value whatever for society, or whether the
same amount of labor might not have been more use-
fully expended, it is to be observed that the several
different systems of modern education uniformly attempt to construct certain predominant, regulative
states, in other words, to create a species of attention.
They begin with extremely simple acts.   Thus, in
certain asylums in the United States, in order to
arouse the attention of idiots, they are taught to put
plugs into a hole, to repeat an air, or to associate a
given word with certain figures, etc.†

*   *   *

Attention—to recapitulate—is an attitude of the
mind ; I would say a *formal* state, if this term were not
generally misemployed. Graphically, we might represent the totality of its normal and morbid manifestations by a straight line, dividing at its two extremities

---

* Esquirol, *Maladies Mentales*, Vol. I, p. 11.
† Séguin, *Traité de l'éducation des idiots*, Paris, 1846 ; Ireland, " Mental
Idiocy."

into two branches. At the centre, let us put ordinary spontaneous attention. Following our imaginary line to the right, in the direction of increasing attention, we find strong spontaneous attention, then pre-occupation, then the weak fixed idea ; the line thereupon branches in the two directions to represent the two extreme degrees—the confirmed fixed idea and ecstasy. Reverting to our starting point, we now turn to the left, in the direction of decreasing intensity. Here we have voluntary attention, at first in the form of an organized habit, then in its general ordinary form, then vacillating, and finally we come to the division into branches corresponding to the two extremes of temporary failure and utter impossibility of attention. Between each form and its adjacent ones, there occur shades which I omit to notice ; but we are able by this manner of representation to comprehend the common origin of all these states and their unity of composition.

CONCLUSION.

I.

WE have endeavored to establish, in the present work, the thesis, that the immediate and necessary condition of attention in all its forms is interest—that is, natural or artifical emotional states—and that, further, its mechanism is motory. Attention is not a faculty, a special power, but a predominant *intellectual state*, resulting from complex causes that induce a shorter or longer adaptation. We have dwelt sufficiently upon the part sustained by movements and we need not here revert to the subject ; but it will be to advantage to make a short 'study of the emotional states that awaken and sustain attention. Up to this point we have limited ourselves to the statement of their functions, and have said nothing of their nature.

We do not intend, here, to present to the reader, incidentally and by way of digression, a psychology of the feelings. I merely propose to show, that from the simple fact that attention always depends upon emotional states, it *in radice* comprises motor elements. And our principal thesis, in this new manner, will be once more justified.

In the first place we must discard the generally accredited opinion which takes the basis of our emotional life to be constituted of pleasure and pain. Pleasure and pain are nothing more than effects, results, indications, signs, which show that certain appetites, inclinations, and tendencies are either satisfied or thwarted. They represent merely the superficial, final part of the phenomenon—the only part that enters consciousness. They are the hands of the clock, not its works. The true causes of emotional life must be sought lower down—in the innermost and deepest recesses of the organism. Feelings, emotions, and passions have their primordial source in the organic, vegetative activity. Whatever comes from the heart, the various vessels, the digestive, the respiratory, the sexual organs, in a word, from the viscera, constitutes the primal subject-matter of sensibility ; just as everything that comes from the external senses, constitutes the primal subject-matter of intelligence : and just as, physiologically, vegetative life precedes animal life, which rests upon it, so also, psychologically, emotional life precedes intellectual life, which rests upon it. The states designated as needs, appetites, inclinations, tendencies, and desires, are the direct and immediate results of every animal organization. They constitute the true basis of emotional life. With Spinoza we say: "Appetite is the very essence of man. . . . . Desire is appetite with consciousness of self. . . . . From this it results, that the foundation of effort, volition, appetite, and desire, is not the fact that a person has adjudged a thing to be good ; but, on the contrary, a person deems a thing good *because* he tends toward it from effort, will, appetite, and desire." At bottom, pleasure is not sought for its own sake, or pain for its own sake avoided ; for it is clear, that we cannot seek or avoid what we do not know. Only the animal, capable of experience, that is, of memory and reflection, is able to seek or avoid, for their own sakes, agreeable and disagreeable states already experienced. The many psychologists, accordingly, who define sensibility as "the faculty of experiencing pleasure and pain," who consequently regard these two phenomena as essential characteristics, do not descend to the true origin of emotional life. To give a definition that contemplates the cause and not the effects, we ought to say, " It is the faculty of desiring, and *consequently* of experiencing pleasure and pain."* And further, these cravings, appetites, desires (for brevity we shall henceforth designate them simply " tendencies ") are themselves effects of organization : they are the immediate expression of its permanent or transitory modes of being.

It would be useless to adduce a mass of data and arguments to establish the fact that pleasure and pain depend upon tendencies, which in turn depend upon the organism. To proceed rapidly and convin-

* Incidentally I use their terminology, yet without accepting it.

cingly, it will suffice to make a brief excursion into the
pathology of the emotional states.   We shall see the
agreeable and the disagreeable vary exactly as tendencies do.   Where the normal man with normal inclinations will find pleasure, the abnormal man with abnormal inclinations will encounter pain, and *vice versa.*
Pleasure and pain follow tendency, as the shadow follows the body.

Let us begin with the tendencies connected with
the fundamental function of nutrition.   Everybody
knows of the "cravings" of pregnancy.   As the consequence of poor nutrition in the first months, there
are produced digestive, circulatory, and secretory
perturbations, which reveal themselves in the form of
strange appetites and depraved tastes.   The afflicted
persons will eat clay, straw, tobacco, soot, etc.   The
same tendencies are met with in certain hysterical,
chlorotic, and neuropathic subjects.   The beginning
of insanity is sometimes marked by an eccentric and
disorderly alimentary course.   There have been instances of people who had a pronounced taste for
spiders, toads, and worms.   Still lower are found
cases of "coprophagy" and "scatophagy."   It was
found necessary, in the ward of a hospital, to watch a
certain patient, in order to prevent him from swallow-
ing the contents of the spittoons.*   The same perver-
sion occurs in respect of the sense of smell.   Certain
neuropathic subjects find the smell of roses disagreeable, but relish the odor of valerian or asafœtida.

Is it necessary to dwell at length upon the deviations and perversions of the sexual instincts ?   Here
instances abound.   Even after making ample allowance for imitation, for willful debauchery, and for that

* Campbell, in *Journal of Mental Science*, July, 1886.

which comes rather from the head (from the imagination) than from the senses, there still remains an abundant harvest. The same conclusion always asserts itself : change the organization, and you will change the tendencies, and, moreover, you will change the position of pleasure and of pain : the latter, accordingly, are but phenomena of indication, or signs to the effect that the necessities of the organisms, whatsoever they be, are satisfied or thwarted.

If it be thought that the inclinations I have just enumerated are of too physiological a nature, I may cite the great group of irresistible impulsions which includes the ungovernable craving for drink, the unconquerable impulse to steal, to practice incendiarism, to kill, to commit suicide. To the consciousness of the individual, these impulsions are without cause, without reasonable motives, and that is so because their true cause, the conditions of their genesis are beneath consciousness ; it knows only the results of this unconscious work. These irresistible impulses are manifested in very dissimilar forms. The most trifling examples are as instructive to psychology as the most truculent. Thus, "onomatomania" is a species of aberration very inoffensive to human society ; the finding out of the name of some stranger, read by chance in a newspaper, torments the patient, and brings with it insomnia and anxiety. How many names do we not all forget, and yet we never concern ourselves further about it. But here an abnormal, absurd impulsion arises. Until the patient accomplishes his purpose, the impulse causes him pain. When he has done so there is pleasure. Let us also remark, that whenever an irresistible impulsion of any kind (to theft, murder, etc.) has been realized, there comes a moment of relaxation, of satisfaction.

These various morbid manifestations have been accurately studied in recent times. They are regarded as symptoms of one and the same cause, namely, degeneration. And the result is that we ever find the same interconnection : anomaly in organization, anomaly in the tendencies that express it, and anomaly in the position of pleasure and of pain.

This being admitted—that the fundament of emotional life rests in tendencies, whether conscious or not (consciousness in all this playing but a secondary part)—how are we to represent to ourselves these tendencies ? The only positive idea that we can get of them is to consider them as movements (or as inhibitions of movements), be they real or nascent. They enter, thus, into the order of motor phenomena ; in other words, a craving, an inclination, a desire always imply *motor innervation* in some degree or other.

The beast that has seized his prey and is rending it with teeth and claws, has attained his purpose and satisfied his tendencies by the aid of considerable expenditure of movement. Suppose that he does not yet possess his victim, but keeps it in sight, and is lying in wait for it ; then his whole organism will be in the state of extreme tension, ready to act : the movements are not yet carried out, but the slightest impulsion will cause them to pass into action. A weaker degree is where the animal prowls about, seeking by sight and scent some capture, which the hazard of the chase will throw in its path ; this is a state of half-tension, the motor innervation being less strong, and vaguely adapted. Finally, a still weaker degree, the animal is at rest in his den. The vague image of prey, that is, the memory of victims that have been devoured, traverses his mind ; the motor element assumes only a nascent, a very slight, degree of intensity, and does not manifest itself through any visible movement. It is certain, that between these four degrees there is continuity, and that there is always in play a motor element, with a simple difference of degree of intensity.

The example last chosen is intentionally roughly drawn, to make things clear. We might just as well have taken love, aversion, or fear, setting out from their most tumultuous motor manifestations, and, through successive weakenings, which actually are met with in real life, finally reducing them to a purely internal state that is only an extremely feeble motory innervation, or movement in the nascent condition.

The tendency, thus, is bound up in a physiological phenomenon, which imparts to it a body. It is no longer "a state of the soul," of a mysterious and transcendent character. Proclivities, inclinations, desires—all these words and their synonyms signify a nascent or miscarried movement, according as it is capable of being evolved to its extreme limit, or is obliged to undergo arrest of development. The state of concomitant consciousness may indifferently appear or disappear ; the tendency may be conscious or unconscious ; yet the motor innervation none the less remains as the fundamental element.

We arrive, accordingly, at the following conclusion: attention depends upon emotional states ; emotional states are reducible to tendencies ; tendencies are fundamentally movements (or arrested movements) and may be conscious or unconscious. Attention, both spontaneous and voluntary, is accordingly, from its origin on, bound up in motory conditions.

II.

It now remains for us to offer a few remarks on the most general physical conditions of attention.   If we closely observe men as they are, taken as a whole, and not the drilled and cultured minds—as psychologists almost always do—we shall surely find that spontaneous attention, and above all voluntary attention, are exceptional states.   Eliminate first the general routine of life—that enormous mass of habits that move us like automatons, with vague and intermittent states of consciousness. Eliminate the periods of our mental life in which we are purely passive simply because the order and succession of our states of consciousness are given to us from without, and because their serial connection is imposed upon us : as when we read a book of average interest, work at a manual occupation, or at anything involving a succession of acts in a fixed order.   Eliminate that state of relative intellectual repose in which people "think of nothing," that is, wherein the states of consciousness have neither intensity nor clear determination : intellectual *nonchalance*, reverie in all its degrees.   Eliminate finally all states of passion and violent agitation, with their disorderly flux and diffusion of movements.   And having made these eliminations, with perhaps a few others, we may then credit to the general account of attention that which remains.   In this general account, the cases of spontaneous attention make up by far the greater number ; the clear and indisputable cases of voluntary attention constitute the minority ; in many men and women they amount almost to nothing.   The psychological reasons of this difference we have at-

tempted to give.   But we have also incidentally noted
the fact of common experience that in the state of
fatigue, the state of exhaustion, attention is very difficult, often impossible, and always without duration.
And the reason is, that attention, by its very nature,
more than any other intellectual state requires a great
expenditure of physical force, which has to be produced under particular conditions.

Let us once more recall to mind, that it exists only
through a limitation of the field of consciousness,
which is equivalent to saying, that *physically* it presupposes the putting into activity of a limited part of
the brain.   It matters not whether we conceive this
part as a localized region, or—which is more probable
—as formed of different elements, spread throughout
the mass of the encephalon, and working in harmony
to the exclusion of the others.   The normal state of
consciousness supposes diffusion, with the work of the
brain diffused.   Attention supposes concentration, with
the work of the brain localized.   When the brain passes
from the normal state to the state of deep attention,
this transition is the analogue of what happens when
instead of carrying a weight on our shoulders we are
compelled to support it with one of our fingers.   This
work, falling wholly upon one portion of the organ,
can only take place through a rapid transformation of
potential or reserve energy into actual, kinetic energy.
All physiological work is the product of chemical
action, performed in the organism, which in turn
owes its origin to food and oxygen.   This production
of work, resulting from nutrition, is far from being constant.   It is unavoidable that in debilitated persons
the work of reserve gives way, and that consequently
exhaustion soon sets in.   Even among persons unusu-

ally gifted, the accumulated capital is quickly expended, if attention be deep and long-continued. It seems, accordingly, that the last physical condition exacted by attention, consists in what physiologists call dynamogeny, that is, according to Brown-Séquard's definition, " the power which certain parts of the nervous system possess of suddenly evoking an augmentation of activity, through a purely dynamic influence." This author * reports the observation of a young girl, who every Sunday at the sound of a bell was thrown into ecstasy, and who for twelve successive hours would stand upright on the polished edge of her bed, supporting herself only by her toes and a small part of the soles of her feet, and could not be disturbed from her immobility by three violent electro-magnetic shocks. She spent the rest of the week in bed, exhausted, almost incapable of movement. To accomplish this difficult feat for half a day, without interruption, would demand a prodigious power of action in the motory apparatus. Is it not probable, that cases of extraordinary and prolonged attention require within certain parts of the nervous system a like exceessive activity, which is likewise followed by a period of fatigue and impotency? Dynamogeny, however, is a physiological state the causes of which are as yet so little known that it would prove idle to dwell upon the question, and to draw hence any psychological deductions.

It is further necessary to observe that the preceding remarks only rigorously apply to the *physical* conditions of attention. The terms "work" and "transformation of energy" have a value and significance

---

* " *Dictionaire encycloped. des Sciences médicales, Art. Dynamogenie,*" and " *Gazette Hebdomadaire.*" Jan. 20th, 1852.

only in the order of physical phenomena. The state of consciousness, the internal occurrence (whatever idea we may form of it) is not commensurable with the former. The "psychic force," of which certain authors speak, is but a metaphor, unless by it are understood the physical conditions of a state of consciousness—and these only. To maintain that a powerful attention depends upon the possibility of a transformation of potential energy into actual energy, is simply to indicate one of its fundamental, material conditions, and nothing more.

*   *   *

In concluding this study of attention, there are numerous practical consequences that might well be pointed out. That task I decline. My sole aim has been, to analyze its mechanism. The subject, in my estimation, has nowhere been treated as its importance demands. This it has been my endeavor to do, and, in agreement with the doctrine of evolution, to show that voluntary attention is nothing else than a higher and extreme form—the result of lower forms rising from half-conscious and half-unconscious processes.

www.ingramcontent.com/pod-product-compliance
Lightning Source LLC
Chambersburg PA
CBHW030625270326
41927CB00007B/1307